6-26-01

One Minute Journaling

by Joanna Campbell Slan

Books by Joanna Slan:

Scrapbook Storytelling (EFG)

Storytelling with Rubber Stamps (EFG)

Quick & Easy Pages (EFG)

I'm Too Blessed to Be Depressed (EFG)

Using Stories and Humor: Grab Your Audience (Allyn & Bacon)

Contributions by Joanna Slan

"Directory Assistance" **4th Course of Chicken Soup for the Soul**

"Damaged Goods" **Chicken Soup for the Couple's Soul**

"Climbing the Stairway to Heaven" **Chicken Soup for the Soul at Work**

"The Scar" **Chicken Soup for a Woman's Soul, Vol. II**

"And I Almost Didn't Go", "The Last of the Big, Big Spenders" **Chocolate for a Woman's Soul**

"United States of Motherhood" **Chocolate for a Woman's Heart**

Chicken Soup for the Expectant Mother's Soul

Cover and inside pages:
Photography and design:
VIP Graphics
(314) 535-1117

Hand sketch:
Bill Perry

Dedicated to Joshua David Newell
August 8, 1976 to July 6, 1981

*This book is for Josh, who taught me to cherish life—
even when all we have are small snips of time.
Wherever you are, you are near to me always.
Thank you for all you taught me.*

Acknowledgements. Thanks to the independent (in business and in spirit) scrapbook stores who have provided such valuable feedback and support over the last two years.

Scrapbook Storytelling: One Minute Journaling
Copyright © 2001 Joanna Campbell Slan

First Edition. Printed and bound in the United States of America.
04 03 02 01 00   5 4 3 2 1

Library of Congress Control Number 2001088691
ISBN: 1-930500-03-3

Trademarks and Copyrights. Scrapbook Storytelling is a trademark of Paperdolls of St. Louis. Throughout this book, the author and publisher have made every attempt to respect copyrighted and trademarked material. In the case of accidental infringement, please contact the publisher to make corrections for future reprints and editions. For instances when the trademark symbol has not been used, the author and publisher had no intention of infringing upon that trademark. Manufacturers and suppliers and their trademarks are listed on the Web site, www.scrapbookstorytelling.com.

Publisher:
EFG, Inc.
savetales@aol.com
www.scrapbookstorytelling.com

Distributed to the trade by:
Betterway Books & North Light Books
Imprints of F&W Publications
1507 Dana Ave., Cincinnati, OH 45207
(800) 289-0963; *fax:* (513) 531-4082

Contents

? STORY STARTERS

In the Story Starter boxes, I'll be asking you questions that may spark an idea for a family story that you haven't yet scrapbooked.

Remember, do the "doable deed." If you only have a minute, use it to get part of your journaling started or completed.

Boxes with the stopwatch icon appear throughout this book. In them, you'll find One Minute Journaling tips to help you break down writing into doable tasks.

Welcome to One Minute Journaling

Years ago I was hired by a company that specialized in teaching adults how to write. After an extensive train-the-trainer program, I was ready to teach my first class. But before my teacher and I parted, she tapped me on the shoulder and said, "I saved the most important piece for last. Listen closely…"

She leaned over and looked me square in the eyes, "Most adults are afraid to write. They've been yelled at, embarrassed and graded so much that the idea of writing terrifies them. Your job is to help them get over that fear."

She was right. I met wonderful, competent and smart people who cried at the thought of writing. Most of the students arrived the first day with pencil, notebook and an overwhelming feeling of failure, a hangover from their past. Once my students got started, they were good writers. Many went on to be terrific, and all could arrange information in an understandable, useful form. The joy and relief on their faces as they experienced success motivated me to continue looking for ways to make writing fun and easy.

You, too, can write. This book includes my favorite ideas and skills from my scrapbook convention workshops and in-store classes. The best news of all is that scrapbookers keep e-mailing and telling me, "They work!"

You've Got Mail.
Still convinced you can't journal? At least you can save what other people write with this fun mailbox page. Go to www.-scrapbookstorytelling.com for the pattern (under the "Templates" button).

SLAN
Chesterfield MO 63005

You've got mail!

Not Interested in the Pep Talk? Start Here

The two major pieces of information you need to know:

1) You'll write with more speed and ease if you divide your scrapbooking into two tasks: page layout and journaling.

   Journaling is a left brain activity, and page layout uses the right side of your brain. Once you get in a layout groove, go with it, but leave room on your page to journal at a later time. We call this space SOFJ, Site of Future Journaling, and suggest that you allow space equal to about a half of a photo per page. After you get a pile of pages with SOFJs, sit down and write your journaling for these pages all at once.

2) The biggest misconception about writing is that it is a *skill*. The biggest revelation about writing is that it is a *set of skills*.

   That set includes:

   C—Collecting information
   O—Organizing the information
   P—Polishing your composition

This book begins with pages that use the fewest of the COP skills and moves to pages involving the most COP skills. You'll start with the information that comes off the top of your head, then travel to using other people's words, move on to combining your words and theirs, and end up with your own composition. Enjoy!

Still Not Convinced?

That's fine—I live in Missouri, the Show Me State. Let me tell you the other ways I can help, through my Web site, www.scrapbookstorytelling.com:

1) Sign up for free monthly Story Starters to help you stay jazzed about telling your stories.

2) See links to other helpful sites and suppliers.

3) Read articles I've written for Graceful Bee, an on-line scrapbook site at www.gracefulbee.com.

Attitude of Gratitude. Here's proof anyone can write. Inside the pocket is my Thanksgiving "To Do" list. (I bet you made one, too.) I also saved a prayer that I cut from the newspaper that we said for grace and an article about gratitude that I liked. You don't have to write a novel to add a personal touch to your pages.

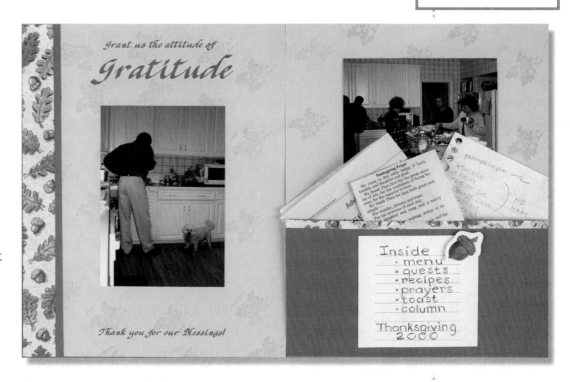

TOOLBOX

SUPPLIES USED

Paper:
Vellum: Paper Adventures
Patterned: Provo Craft

Punches:
Cat: Carl
Moon: McGill

Stamp:
Stampa Rosa

Ink:
Archival Inks by Ranger Industries

Font:
CK Fill In, CK Script

Pencils:
Berol

Other Supplies:
Trimmer by Fiskars
Crimper by Paper Adventures

? STORY STARTERS

Are your friends pet lovers? What do they own? How did they adopt their pets? What does your family say about your pet?

When Elaine's children would complain about Thomas, Elaine would say, "I had him before I had you." That was that. When he died in August of 2000, Elaine was heartbroken. She called him, "An old barn cat," but he was awfully special to her.

Thomas Catus Private Prowler

What can you do to comfort a friend who's lost a pet? In our culture, we recognize the loss of a family member or a co-worker or a peer, but we're sadly behind the curve when it comes to acknowledging how much our pets mean to us. When my friend Elaine lost Thomas, I wanted a way to help her keep his memory alive. She'd given me his photo to use when I was working on pet pages for a special project. All I had to do was remember enough to add journaling, so I started with what I knew.

CRAFTING: *Creating a Scene with Stamps*

◄ **Cut** a 3 ½" x 3 ½" box out of black paper. Cut a 3" x 3" box out of grey paper. Cut the gray box into four equal sections. Put HERMAfix on the back of all the gray sections and adhere them to the black square, spacing them to look like window panes.

Put your "window" on a piece of waste paper and stamp a black tree onto the window panes, taking care to position the stamp so that only a few branches show up in the window. Add a punch of a black cat and a punch of a moon. ▶

◄ **Crimp** a piece of vellum, 3" x 4". Fold it under the top edge and adhere the vellum strip under the black paper of your window. Print out the headline and the journaling box on white paper. Color in the headline. Crop and mat it. Mat the photo. Adhere all of the elements to the page.

A Day Late or a Photo Short?

Only have one photo to work with? Or missing a visual record all together? We don't always have a camera with us when important moments occur. And there are times when the click of a shutter would be an unwelcome intrusion. But don't let that stop you from illustrating what matters to you.

Use embellishments or journaling boxes as the focal point of your page. Here, the photo of Thomas is slightly overexposed, but the embellishment of the cat in the night time window sets the perfect mood for saying goodbye.

Tip!

Attached to Vellum

Adhering vellum is tricky. The adhesive often shows through. One way to get around the problem is by doing what I did here— fold over the vellum and adhere the folded edge to the backside of the embellishment.

Note: In Paper Adventure's book *Creativity Taking Flight: Parchlucent*, Patti Swoboda notes that vellum is actually a term for the finish of a paper. However, since the word *vellum* is used by scrapbookers to mean translucent paper of any kind, I use the term this way throughout this book.

Tip!

Mix It Up

For stunning pages that really tell a story, don't be afraid to mix techniques. This page combines paper piecing (the window), stamping (the tree), punch art (the cat and moon), and vellum.

WRITING: *Starting with What You Know*

> Write down what you know about a topic. Think: WHO, WHAT, WHEN, WHERE, WHY and HOW.
>
> ❧ AND ❧
>
> Recheck what you've written with another person who knows your topic.

Indeed, you probably have more memories in the 'file cabinets' of your mind than you may at first realize.

—Jay Amberg and Mark Larson

When was the last time you opened those mental files and looked inside? Instead of despairing of having perfectly kept paper journals, say a hearty "Thank you" and consider what you've already absorbed and stored in your mind.

Gently pry inside those files. Don't expect them to yield all their treasures at one sitting. Begin with a blank piece of paper and start to doodle. Yes, you read right. *Doodle.* A blank piece of paper is terrifying, but a doodle will quickly fill the space and get the ink and your juices flowing. Write whatever comes to mind.

Here's a trick I rely on constantly when I write: Play your mental tape recorder and listen to your subject talk. Once you can "hear" a voice in your head, you've connected in a sensory way to your topic. I imagined listening to Elaine in those panicky days when Thomas was actually in the process of dying. I recalled her outpouring of concern for him.

Once I had her voice, I had a few remembrances of Thomas. I jotted them down and kept them by the phone. The next time we talked, I asked her how she was recovering from his death, and then slipped in a few questions. "Didn't you tell your kids when they complained that Thomas was there first?"

I used Elaine's words to correct mine. By adding the date of Thomas' death, I had what I needed for a journaling box. The headline I used is also the title of a wonderful movie, *Goodnight, Mister Tom.*

BONUS TIP #1:

Keep a file of old catalogs of videos and music that come in the mail. When you need a page title, skim through the catalogs for ideas.

Repetition is the Mother of Learning and Remembering

You'll be amazed at how repeating a person's own words back to her prompts more information. (It's an old, old interviewer's trick. Remember it when you need to keep your counsel!)

When I had an interview show on television, I repeated what my guests said to me as a way of buying time to think up a good question. Then, accidentally, I learned that we are all comforted by having our words repeated to us. In fact, psychologists have a fancy term for this. They call it the reflexive technique.

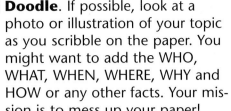

Doodle. If possible, look at a photo or illustration of your topic as you scribble on the paper. You might want to add the WHO, WHAT, WHEN, WHERE, WHY and HOW or any other facts. Your mission is to mess up your paper!

Walk away from your notes for at least an hour, and preferably, a day. Add any new thoughts.

Recopy your work so you can read it. Put your information in a logical sequence. Make notes of any questions you have. Gently check with your subject to see if you need to make revisions.

Create a final draft. Type the notes into your computer. Set the margins for the space you've allotted on the page. Print out a rough copy. Adjust the margins if needed. Print out a final copy.

The Dearest Gift

Scrapbook pages make the ultimate gifts. You are helping someone else preserve what they hold dear. You are creating a one-of-a-kind piece of art. You have noticed what matters to another human being. Gift giving doesn't get much better than this.

Down Time is the Right Time

There's a slightly technical name for the "down time" when you walk away from your work. It's called *fermentation*. While you do another task, your subconscious takes over your writing. Since your subconscious has the keys to all your mental file cabinets, don't be shocked when she digs up really, really choice stuff. But go easy on her. She has a lot of filing to do, and no one ever catches up on filing.

Writing and the Need to Know

If you wait until you have everything you need to know before you write, you'll never write a word. Trust me. Writing explores rather than dictates. You must start somewhere, and the best place is exactly where you are. William Zinsser said, "American children have long been taught to visualize a composition as a finished edifice, its topic sentences all in place, its spelling correct, its appearance tidy. Only lately has there been an important shift... from product to process."

If you think you can't write, you're a victim of product. You think you can't produce a perfect polished piece in one sitting. Surprise! The best writers can't and don't. Writing happens in bits and pieces, fits and starts. I put down what I know. I realize what I don't know. I get more information. I ask questions. I return to my struggling sentences and prop them up. I prune them. And, hey, baby, I'm writing. And so will you. Trust the process and take it one step at a time. Most of the steps will only take one minute, but the results will stand the test of time.

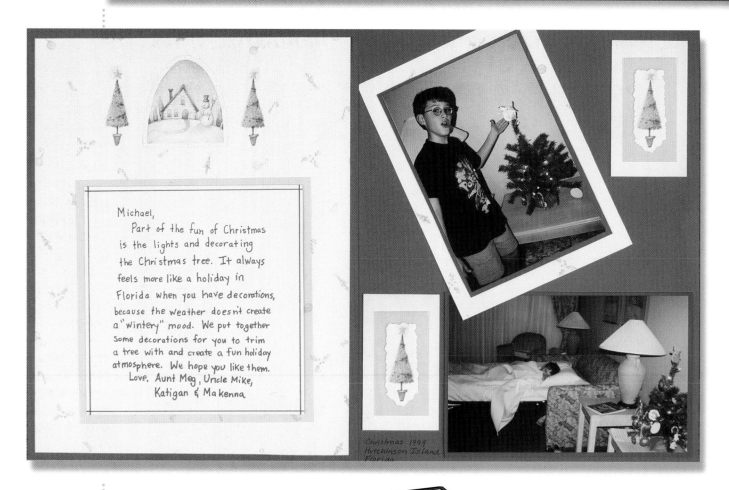

Michael,
    Part of the fun of Christmas is the lights and decorating the Christmas tree. It always feels more like a holiday in Florida when you have decorations, because the weather doesn't create a "wintery" mood. We put together some decorations for you to trim a tree with and create a fun holiday atmosphere. We hope you like them.
    Love, Aunt Meg, Uncle Mike, Katigan & Makenna

Christmas 1999
Hutchinson Island
Florida

? STORY STARTERS

How have fads and trends affected your celebrations? What do you do on holidays that sets your family apart from others?

TOOLBOX

SUPPLIES USED

Paper:	Solid green paper by Canson
	Imprintable source unknown
	Parchlucent by Paper Adventures
Lettering:	Handwritten note from Margaret
Pens:	Fibracolor

Over the Intercoastal and Through the Palms We Go

My whole family has migrated to Florida. Since my son Michael is an only child, he loves spending time with his cousins. So each year, we trek from St. Louis to Florida for the holidays and stay at a hotel on Hutchinson Island. Making sure all our gifts arrive has priority over bringing along ornaments. Fortunately, my sister Margaret thinks of everything. She makes sure we have our own pint-size Christmas tree. In 1999, she even put together a package of ornaments guaranteed to please Michael because they were all Pokémon characters.

CRAFTING: *Resizing and Copying Handwritten Text*

◀ **Mat** the photos first with a solid color paper. Add a mat of patterned paper underneath the solid mat.

Cut an image of the tree from paper and trim it with deckle edge scissors. Mat the photo with vellum. Mat it again on solid paper. Add the journaling box. Affix all the elements to the page. ▶

◀ **Use** an archival pen to make the border around the journaling box. Mat the large journaling box with vellum. Trim $1/4$" off each side of the page of patterned paper. Mat it onto solid cardstock. Attach the journaling box to the page.

A Rose is a Rose

What you think of as "stationery," the paper products world calls "imprintables." These papers typically feature a border or design at the top and a space in the center for a message. Imprintables can be used for accent paper, background paper or embellishments. On this particular page, I used the paper in all three ways.

Take Dictation

The colors you use on your page must be dictated by the colors in your photos or the pages won't work visually. The color of our hotel room overshadowed the red and green of Michael's tree, so a lot of my stock of Christmas paper clashed with these pictures. For best results, take your photos with you when you make the selections of background paper and embellishments.

Paper Weights

Like regular paper, scrapbooking paper comes in a variety of weights and textures. *Cardstock* is what scrapbookers call heavy-weight solid colored paper. Cardstock is perfect for background paper on the pages because it can support the additional weight of embellishments. Light weight paper does better for embellishments that need fine cutting and punching.

Vellum is both light weight and see-through, but it isn't always a sturdy paper. Parchlucent, a vellum by Paper Adventures, is both crisp and translucent, making it useful for such techniques as embossing, punching and layering. Parchlucent handles ink from desktop printers well—a real bonus because some vellums smear easily.

WRITING: *Recopying Correspondence*

Locate a hand-written note from a family member.

❧ *AND/OR* ❧

Make a reduced copy of a hand-written note.

No passion in the world is equal to the passion to alter someone else's draft.

—H.G. Wells

So few of us take the time to handwrite anything these days! Each piece I receive from a friend or family member gets squir-reled away like the precious artifact it is. Unfortunately, these missives aren't always the size I need or the color of ink I'd like. That's why I love to recopy them for use on my pages.

Here are ways to get the look you want:

1) **Color copy the piece**. Reduce or enlarge the element to the size you want for the page. Since color copy-ing is expensive, I often play with copy sizes in black and white first, then I make my color copy. Even if the piece you are copying is only black and white, make a color copy. Your final piece will be more realistic.

2) **Scan your piece**. Once the data is in your computer, you can size the piece as you wish. You can even print out several sizes to play with as you lay out the page.

3) **Make a black and white copy**. Size it as you wish. Then put the black and white copy on the light box and trace the words in archival ink on archival paper. You'll recopy the handwriting as it is, but you'll be able to change the size and color while guaranteeing archival safety.

4) **Photograph your document**. This is more cumbersome, but if the paper isn't flat, this might be a good way to copy an image.

Of course, if you want to use the piece as is, simply spray it with a de-acidifying spray such as Archival Mist or put the piece in an archival protective pocket.

Remember, tedious as it is compared to e-mail or phone calls, we should all take the time to write our loved ones a handwritten note at least once in a while.

Little Things Mean a Lot

Funny, but once someone is gone, the smallest notes from them mean so much. When my grandmother died, I found a 2 ½" x 2 ½" note on which she'd written my name and phone number. I have other notes from Grandma, but seeing my vital information in her hand was so moving. Of course, I kept the scrap, and a page in my remembrance album will spotlight this tiny piece of fiber and ink. Do you keep snips of correspondence? Notes? Post-it notes? Grocery lists? Greeting card messages? A few lines on the back of an envelope: "Be home soon. Went to pick up the boys. Love…" These are the precious items in life.

◀ **Measure** your original piece of correspondence. Measure the new space for your correspondence. Divide the small number (new space) by the big number (original) to get a percentage. Reduce your original correspondence to that percentage. Check the size of your final piece. Adjust and recopy it if necessary.

Put your photocopied piece on a light box. Cover it with a piece of archival paper. Tack both down with a Post-it note. Copy the photocopied piece with an archival pen. ▶

◀ **Mat** the journaling box with vellum. Trim 1/4" off all the edges of the patterned paper. Affix the journaling box to the page. Attach all elements to the page.

Reduction Redux

Remember: When you reduce the side dimensions, the top and bottom will shrink by the same amount. A 10" x 10" note reduced to 70% will be 7" on all four sides. A 10" x 8" note reduced to 70% will measure 7" x 5.6 ".

See the Light

I'm amazed that more scrapbookers don't own light boxes. I use mine all the time to recopy handwriting, to copy fonts, and for paper piecing. In a pinch, you can tape your papers up to a bright window and use natural light to copy them, but since I use mine so often, I'd say, "Buy one." Over the long haul, they actually save you money because you can do so much with them.

A Quick Trip Around the Border

Adding an inked border to your pages doesn't take much time, but produces a plethora of visual pizzazz. Here's how:

Put a ruler across the top of the new journaling box, about 1/4" down from the top edge. Draw a line with an archival pen. Wipe off the ruler edge with a paper towel or a tissue (to prevent smearing) then repeat the process. Repeat this on all sides to make a border.

Now, try these variations:
- Use two colors of ink and draw a double line on each side.
- Alternate thick and think pens for your double lines.
- Spread the double lines apart and add ink dots in between.
- Forget the ruler and make your lines wobbly.
- Draw your lines at the edges of the paper rather than indenting them 1/4" inside as suggested above.
- Use a border template and make curvy or wavy lines.

SUPPLIES USED

Paper:
Vellum paper by
Paper Pizazz

Baby paper source
unknown

Ink:
Ink jet printer

Punch:
ACCO

Paper trimmer:
Fiskars

? STORY STARTERS

*How did you know that
new little bundle finally
made an appearance?
What important e-mail
announcements have
you received? Print out
e-mails you want to
keep as scrapbooking
reference material.*

Eliza and the E-mail

Nancy became pregnant shortly after she moved here, which was right about the time we met. Our family followed her pregnancy with great anticipation. When the e-mail followed the phone confirmation of Eliza's birth, I tucked the e-mail away with plans to make a page.

By the time I got around to the page, Eliza was nearly a year old. Nancy read the journaling on this page and said, "Where did you get that?" We laughed when I showed her the e-mail.

CRAFTING: *Adding Vellum with Paper Ties*

◄ **Use** a craft knife to cut around the outside of an art element on the background paper. Slide a photo under the art. Use archival tape on the backside to secure the photo.

Paper Ribbon

Paper ribbons add a splash of color and texture to your page. Simply cut the strips of paper into narrow "ribbons" and treat them like you would fabric.

(Remember to pull them gently and to use a medium weight paper.)

Print out the finished copy of journaling. Trim the journaling box. Adhere the box to a wide mat. Punch two holes about 1" apart vertically, on the left and right sides of the mat. ▶

Properly Pastel

Turn any bright color to pastel with an overlay of white vellum. (The addition of white to any color makes the color a pastel.) Here I used dotted Swiss because I liked the "girly" feel of the tiny dots. Although they don't show up much against the white journaling box, they make a pretty pattern on the rose hued mat.

◄ **Cut** a piece of vellum the same size as your entire journaling box and mat. Mark and punch holes in the vellum to match the holes in the mat it. Cut two thin ($1/8$") strips of paper and run them through the holes. Tie them together to secure the vellum to the mat. Adhere all the elements.

Colors, Patterns and Bears, Oh My!

The colors for this page come directly from the blanket Eliza is lying on in the photo. For best results, always pull design and color elements from your photos when choosing paper and embellishments.

Notice, too, that Eliza's head is larger than the head of the teddy bear and nearly as large as the size of the toy block. If her head were smaller, she'd be dwarfed by the page elements. If her head were larger, the elements would not have formed a strong visual triangle which draws your eyes to Eliza's sweet face. Play with several sizes of patterns when you work on your pages. But remember, as a general rule, smaller prints are easier to work with.

WRITING: *Taking Information from E-Mail*

Remember why the good Lord made your eyes. Pla-gi-a-rise!

—Tom Lehrer

Edit an e-mail from a friend.
❧ *OR* ❧
Keystroke into your computer an edited e-mail.

In an interview with *Savvy Traveler* Rudy Maxa, author of *Mosquito Coast* Paul Theroux talked about writing his first travel book. He noted that he was so unsure of what he was doing (he had never written a travel book before) that he saved everything. Every scrap of paper, every brochure, every note, every registration form, everything stayed with him until he wrote the book.

Theroux wasn't sure what he would need and neither are you. Hang on to those e-mails. When you keep written matter, you can recycle the information in countless ways on your pages.

Your e-mail correspondence counts as one often overlooked source of scrapbook journaling starts. Consider:

1) **Broadcast e-mails**. These usually announce a change in status, address or family members.

2) **E-mail newsletters**. One brings me great new recipes, another shares wacky happenings, and yet another has great quotations. I like this paper-free method of jogging scrapbooking skills so much I've started my own. You can sign up for Story Starters at www.scrapbookstory-telling.com I'll share fresh ways to tell and preserve your family stories on a monthly basis.

3) **On-going conversations**. My friend Terri lives in Wisconsin, and our visits are infrequent. I try to use my e-mail missives to her as an electronic diary of my life. Terri always asks good questions about what's up, so I'm inspired to share more than a superficial, "We're fine."

4) **Family correspondence**. One year my three sisters and I coordinated a Thanksgiving meal in Indiana from the states of Missouri and Florida. Family correspondence for our clan is usually task- and event-specific, and this batch of e-mail now resides in the pocket of a scrapbook page. (See the scrapbook page on page 5.)

Hang on to the e-mails that cross your desk, and you'll never have to start writing from absolute zero.

A Bundle of Joy Comes to Other Folks' Homes

Michael is destined to be an only child. That doesn't mean we don't have lots of children in our lives to enjoy. My friends' children and my sisters' children bring great pleasure to my life. Why restrict yourself to pages of your own kids? When the neighbor's daughter and her friend opened a lemonade stand, I marched right out with my money—and my camera. Such a hoot! There's so much to enjoy about life every day if we'd just open ourselves to the possibilities. If it takes a village to raise a child, certainly it takes a cluster of scrapbookers to save all those lovely memories.

Print out your original e-mails and keep them filed by topic. If you are positive you will later reuse an e-mail, save it as a file in your computer program.

Edit the e-mails as necessary. Type them into your computer.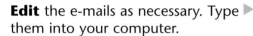

Set the margin guidelines and print out a draft of your journaling. Check to see that the spacing is correct. Adjust it. Print out another rough draft to check again. Print a final draft on archival paper.

Trim the archival copy. Mat it and adhere it to the page. Save your journaling file in your computer.

Nice Save

I don't always save my journaling. When I don't save it, I need it. I'll find out that I made a mistake, or I'll want to make an update. Sure, saving takes up room on your computer, but you may find it worthwhile to waste space, not time.

Habit Forming

Lots of people get in the habit of writing their e-mails in abbreviations and all lower case letters. That's a bad idea. Our spelling ability naturally declines with age and exposure to mistakes, experts say. Why speed the process by allowing yourself to be sloppy? Habits are hard to make but harder to break. Why not cultivate the habit of good grammar?

Printing Your Journaling in Color

Here are some tips for using a color printer to create colored type on archival paper. (It's worth the time it takes to experiment.)

1) **Be sure your type is legible**. Colors other than black may be hard to read. If this happens, switch to bold-face type because it is thicker than regular type. This is especially helpful if you use a narrow type face such as Garamond, MS Line Draw or Dauphin.

2) **Final type color is combination of ink and paper**. Red type on yellow paper is slightly orange because ink and paper work *together* to determine the final color.

3) **Papers have varying porosity**. Your ink may smear if the paper is not porous (because the ink will sit on top and not dry quickly). Shiny papers aren't porous. If the paper is highly porous, the ink may wick out (and look blurry).

SUPPLIES USED

Paper:
Memories Forever

Stamp:
Acorn by Rubber
Stamps of America

Ink:
ColorBox

Chalk:
Decorating Chalks by
Craft-T Products

Watercolor Pencils:
Derwent

What scenic wonder inspires you? Do you have any outstanding local trees or plants? What makes them interesting? What is their history?

The Tree of Life

Perhaps this has happened to you. Perhaps you too have passed a site of interest, saying to yourself, "Next time. I'll stop to see it next time." Our family has visited South Carolina for years, and we never took the time to stop and look at Angel Oak, outside of Charleston. This year, with my son's friend Kip as our guest, we made the time. The boys were enchanted. The tree enthralled them. They walked around and around the massive trunk, speculating on all the history the tree had known.

CRAFTING: *Using an Ink Pad to Mat*

◄ **Stamp** acorns onto strips of paper. Journal on archival paper and cut it to size. Drag the edges of the journaling box and stamped strips over the ink pad to color them. Smear the paper with chalks to make it look old and weathered.

Mat the journaling box on a background made by sponging ink over paper. ►

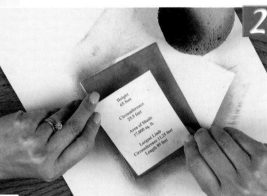

◄ **Paint** an image of the tree on archival paper. Use a light box to trace the lettering of Angel Oak from a brochure. Drag the edges of the paper over an ink pad to color them. Add chalks. Adhere all of the pieces to the pages.

Tip!

On the Edge

Dragging the edge of the paper over an ink pad adds the simplest, cleanest touch of color to your work, a simple and narrow mat. A paper mat would not have been nearly as subtle.

Tip!

Old Paint

You can paint your own images of what you see, even if you are not a seasoned artist. Start with a black and white copy of the image. Trace the photocopy with colored pencils using a light box. Refer to the colored print as you trace the black and white photocopy. Use a variety of media to color in your drawing. Here I used colored pencils, watercolor pencils, and chalk. The whole scene didn't come alive until I added chalk. The soft look of the chalk blended the colors and covered mistakes.

Two- and Three-Page Layouts

As you increase the amount of your journaling , you may wish to move from one- or two-page layouts to two- and three-page spreads. As a result, you'll be able to include more detail without leaving out important information.

Here, I could have used fewer photos, but I wanted the sense of how huge the tree is. I also wanted to show how we all were "engaged" by the sense of discovery the tree awakened in us. By increasing the number of pages to a three-page spread, I was able to tell my story in a satisfying way.

WRITING: *Being Brief with Pull Out Quotes*

Brevity is the soul of wit.

—Shakespeare

> Round up information about your topic.
>
> *❧ OR ❧*
>
> Decide on a sentence stem you'll use to start all your pull out quotes. For example, "Angel Oak is...."

Ironically, you can write more by writing less. Remember your school days and the assignments to write 500 words? Most of us padded our compositions. An editor could have boiled it down to 150 words and not missed an idea.

You can write more (in terms of substance) by writing less (in terms of sheer words). Pull out quotes show you how.

Look at popular magazines and you'll see how one line or remark has been highlighted and enlarged. These are called "pull out quotes."

Scrapbookers can also use this technique by pulling one line of information from any of the material you have gathered. Because pull out quotes aren't narrative, that is they don't try to tell a story, you can start the quotes with the same words over and over. See how I used the words "Angel Oak is..."?

Note, too, how the dimensions of Angel Oak are repeated in a box. No attempt is made to turn these words into complete sentences. Instead, only the briefest of labels accompanies the numbers.

Try pull out quotes whenever you have one topic you want to explore on a page. Or use them when the information lends itself easily to simple subject/verb construction sentences, that is, sentences that read, "It is... They are... He is..." This method of writing is terse and straightforward with a lot fewer curves and bends than Angel Oak.

BONUS TIP #2:
A quick cheat sheet of transitional expressions: however, unless, nevertheless, because, since, when, while, after, until, admittedly, on the contrary, but then, then, but, although, in summary, consequently, first, second, third, finally, now, otherwise, once, in the end, to start, so, as a result, on the other hand, therefore, besides, too, all in all, for the most part, generally, usually, in the long run, in short, at any rate, still, in any case, rather, yet, afterward, at the same time, later on, next, by the way, for example, for instance, and in conclusion.

Making a Smooth Transition Easier

Someone once lectured me that the key to good writing is the transitions. I wouldn't go that far, but I will admit that coming up with smooth transitions is difficult, even for those who write all the time. The Pull Out Quote method speeds your journaling along (as does the Bullet Points method on page 28, or the 20 Things About... method on page 56) because you don't need to use transitions. The graphic look of the information tells the reader: "Hang in here with me, I'm jumping from subject to subject." If transitions are bogging you down, these methods will help you move ahead quickly. Plus, your writing will appear to be seamless.

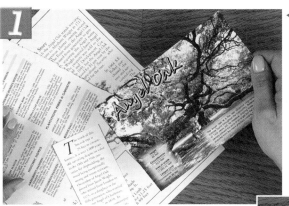

◄ **Sort** through your information to find everything you have about the topic. Decide on a subject/verb sentence structure that you can repeat while adding new information.

Type the pull out quotes into the computer. Space them out on the page. Print out a rough copy and check for spacing. Print out copies on archival paper. Trim.

Flip Cards

Postcards are displayed picture-side out in racks. You'd be tempted then, to purchase the card with the prettiest photo on the front. Instead, flip the card over and read the information on the reverse side. Let that verbiage guide your purchase decision as well as an eye toward the graphic.

Drag the edge of the journaling boxes across the top of an ink pad. Hold the paper at a right angle to the pad. Don't drag the paper too slowly, or the paper will wick up the ink and be too dense. Add chalks as desired. ▶

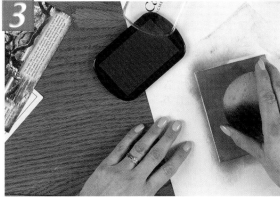

◄ **Cut** a piece of archival paper to mat a journaling box. Tamp a sponge onto an ink pad. Wipe the ink color over the mat. Repeat this until you get the desired shade. Let it dry thoroughly. Affix it to the page.

Sign of the Times

You'll be amazed at what you can do with photos of signs.

1) Signs tell where you were.

2) They give all sorts of useful information.

3) They save you from writing down all that information if you can read it from your photo.

4) They offer you a visual image you may wish to repeat in your page.

My family thought I'd lost my mind when I snapped shots of signs, but they've come around now that they've seen how I use the photos in my pages.

BONUS TIP #3:

To clean your stamps, you could wipe them with baby wipes, but the Stampin' Scrub™ Clean-Up Pad by Stampin' Up! works better. The fibers of the pad get deep into the die to clean out the ink.

Think Before You Ink

To be totally safe in your scrapbook, you need inks that won't fade, won't run if they get wet, and won't ruin your photos. Being the trusting sort that I am, I settle for the manufacturers' claim that the ink is safe for use in scrapbooks. I figure that if my scrapbooks get in a flood, finding them will be more of an issue than reading what's on the pages, but then I moved to St. Louis during the 500-year flood, so I'm a tad cavalier about water over the dam.

TOOLBOX

SUPPLIES USED

Paper:

Nanas: Ever After
Paper Company

Korea: Keeping
Memories Alive

Lettering & Stencils:

Pagerz Template by
ScrapPagerz.com

Puffy Letters Template
by Provo Craft

Journaling Genie by
Chatterbox

Embossing Tool:

The Empressor by
Chatterbox

Chalks:

Decorating Chalks by
Craft-T Products

Pens:

Avery

? STORY STARTERS

*What poems, songs,
sayings or quotations
have been part of your
family lore forever?
Who has shared these
witticisms with you?*

BONUS TIP #4:

Learn about our language. A tinker was an itinerant fixer of household goods. He used "dams," tiny pellets of bread, to help hold solder while fixing holes in pots and pans. When the patch was completed, the dam was of no value. Hence the term "not worth a tinker's dam."

Pass It On

Every family has its sayings, songs, and witticisms that are passed along from one generation to the next. Along the way, we also pick up new material to add to our repertoire. Why not capture these bon mots on a scrapbook page? The "A friend is..." poem is from a wall hanging that my mother has owned for years. My husband and I first heard *Arrirang* in Korea in 1986. I've waited 15 years to find the song's translation. Saving these two tidbits tells a lot about our family. We honor our past but we live as World Citizens reaching out to try to understand our global neighbors.

CRAFTING: *Using Journaling Genie Templates*

◁ *For both pages*: **Lay** archival paper over the Journaling Genie template. Rub the Empressor firmly over the paper. Write on the embossed lines. Cut out the embossed paper and trim it to size.

▽ *For Korea page*: Write verbiage. **Add** chalk, coloring in shades to make the mountains. Emboss the sun and add chalk. Cut a slit in the mountains and tuck in the sun. Affix all elements to the page.

For Nanas: To create the background paper, **tear** one paper in half and then attach it to a full sheet of background paper. Write around the outside of the embossed circle with an archival pen. Draw lines and dots on the embossed lines. Mat the journaling circle inside the circle of contrasting paper.

◁ **Add** the cutout letters to a white page topper strip. Add a border of lines and dots to the page topper. Handwrite the other word and letters. Punch circles for the centers of the top of the **A**'s. Draw in happy faces on the small circles of the inside letters. Affix all the elements to the page.

Clean Up Your Lines Up with JG's Help

Journaling Genie templates give you a simple, raised line on which to write. Since the embossed line is nearly invisible, it serves to guide you without demanding attention. After you finish your handwriting, you can add chalks or markers if you want to make the lines more prominent. The embossed area also adds a subtle texture to the page. Your eyes may not immediately pick up on the fact the embellishment is embossed, but you will notice a certain richness. The Empressor (embossing tool) moves gently and easily over the paper without tearing. There's no need to use a light box, because the rounded ball won't gouge the paper. With the Empressor, you can turn all your letter templates into embossing patterns.

Be Creative with Genie

Journaling Genies come in all sorts of shapes. Let your imagination dictate different ways to use the shapes to create the look you want on your pages. For clues about which shapes to use, look to the pattern of your paper.

Tear 'Em Up

Combine two pieces of paper as I did here to make a unique paper perfect for your page. Remember when you tear, there are two edges—one frayed and one finished. Choose which side you want to be on top. Also note that some papers—like this pattern—have a top and a bottom. Turning these happy faces upside down would have looked pretty silly, but I almost managed to do just that.

WRITING: *Quoting Directly*

In fact, my father told me so many stories about his childhood that it seems in most ways more vivid to me than my own.

—Mary Karr

Label a notebook to hold your camp songs, sayings, poems and so on.

❧ OR ❧

Ask a family member to share a camp song, saying or poem.

❧ OR ❧

Write down a camp song, saying or poem.

True confession: I am the child of a former summer camp counselor. I have probably heard every corny song and saying in the book even though I personally never went to a summer camp like the ones my mother attended. It wasn't until working on these pages that I realized this inventory of camp songs and legends as a rich untapped source for journaling.

After all, whether you sang the songs on long family car trips, chanted the rhymes while marching at band camp, or heard the poems while on your mother's knees, they represent an oral heritage all but forgotten.

Once I recognized the value of these ditties, I dedicated a notebook to them. As one re-surfaced in my mind or on my son's lips after a campout, I scrambled to write down the words.

Short on inherited witticisms? Glean cute sayings from:

T-shirts—look at shops or read catalogs.

Fortune cookies—bonus: these are low calorie sweets.

Old radio shows—sponsors and characters reveled in unforgettable phrases like, "Only the Shadow knows..."

Southerners—At the risk of showing my bias, southern humorists and novelists have a colorful command of our language. Where else can you hear such wisdom as:

Even a blind hog can find an acorn once in a while.

Pretty is as pretty does.

If wishes were horses, then beggars would ride.

Don't care has no house nor home.

Why not start your "witty-speak" notebook today and you, too, can pass on a fireside legacy.

Save the Wit and Share the Memory

Cute sayings only go so far. While they might match the mood of your page perfectly, they still can't tell us the WHO, WHAT, WHEN, WHERE , WHY and HOW behind the pithy phrases.

Witty sayings can take center stage and spotlight your story, but you'll still want to add a sentence or two or a cutline (see definition on page 39) to give more specific information. Fun is great, but we don't want to forget that our purpose is to share memories, not to dumbfound the innocent.

Commit your family sayings, camp songs, witticisms, fortunes from cookies, and other *bon mots* to a notebook.

In the back of the notebook, create an index by subject so you can easily look up topics. Number your pages from front to back.

Copy a witticism in pencil or Journaling Genie Vanishing Ink Pen (VIP) on your page.

VIP Pen Tip

Use your VIP pen anywhere you would use a pencil mark that would later have to be erased. It's a real timesaver.

VIP Vamoose

Here are four things you gotta know about your VIP pen:

1) Air and natural light make the ink disappear. For best results, leave your work out of the page protector and in natural light.

2) Always test your VIP pen on the backside of the paper you are using. If it disappears quickly, you can go over your marks twice. If it takes a long time, write very lightly.

3) Be careful when using it on papers that are dark on one side, and light on the other. If the surface ink hasn't penetrated the paper, the VIP ink may bring up the lighter color underneath.

4) Keep the fiber tip clean. If you write over wet or unstable ink, your VIP ink will be contaminated.

Trace over the VIP or pencil with an archival marker. Allow time for it to dry. If you use the VIP, leave the page out of a page protector for at least 24 hours so the special ink disappears. Erase any pencil marks. Add lines under the writing, if desired.

Coloring Through the Lines...

All my lettering books suggest that I can use a regular, graphite pencil to draw lettering, then color over it with colored pencils. **Wrong.** After years of pencil marks showing through, I found a sentence in a book that explained the problem. Colored pencils are translucent. When you put down a layer of color from the pencils, it simply adds a layer of color over graphite pencil marks. So colored penciling won't cover gray pencil marks.

The solution? Use a VIP pen or draw the letters originally with the colored pencil you intend to use. So, if you want orange letterings, draw the letters lightly in orange. When you color over the orange with the colored pencils, your original guides will disappear.

SUPPLIES USED

Paper:
Keeping Memories
Alive

Fonts:
Headline: CK Concave

Body copy: CK Any-
thing Goes

Stencil:
American Traditional
Stencils

Pens:
Sakura

Watercolor pencils:
Derwent

?STORY STARTERS

*Do you have any "out-
side" pets? Animals
you feed or watch that
never set foot, claw or
paw inside your do-
main? Have you
named them? What do
you find interesting
about these critters?*

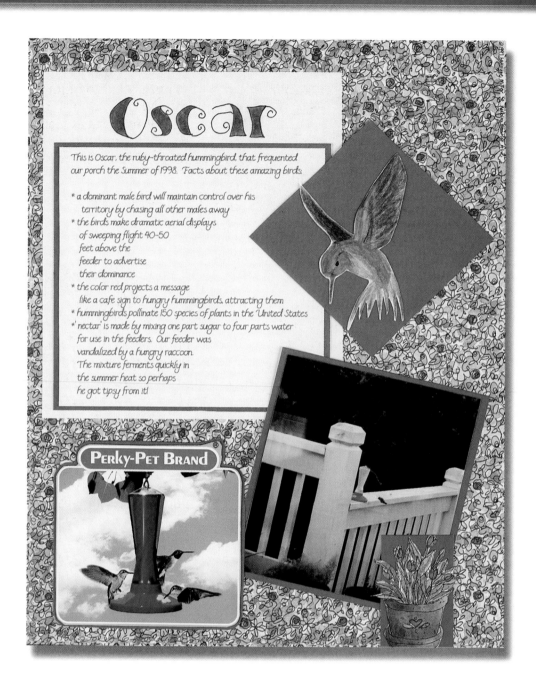

Duck, Quick! It's Oscar Coming in for a Dive

For two summers in a row, the antics of Oscar, the dive-bombing hummingbird have entertained us. Getting his photo was hard, and now I
have a new appreciation for professional photographers who snap
those wonderful close-ups. I did the best I could to capture this tiny, darting
aviator who zoomed his way across our deck all summer. Notice the detail
that the feeder packaging provided. Pieces like this add texture and authori-
ty to our pages. I couldn't photograph the feeder separately because shortly
after these photos, a raccoon chewed it open and drank the sugar water.

CRAFTING: *Working with Stencils and Pencils*

Create a hummingbird embellishment using a stencil, colored pencils and watercolor pencils. Cut it out and mount it on a square of solid paper.

Print out the page title and color in the letters with colored pencils. Print out the journaling and mat it with solid paper. Affix the matted journaling box to the page title.

Spring for a Set
This patterned paper, solid paper and flower pot embellishment all came from Keeping Memories Alive as a set. When you buy coordinated page elements, you save time and frustration trying to match colors and styles.

Crop and mat the photo. Mat the floral embellishment. Cut out the packaging memorabilia and spray it with de-acidifying spray. Let it dry. Mat it. Affix all of the elements to the page.

Play with Pages
I could have put "Oscar" in a square that was mounted parallel with the sides of the page, but by turning the mat so it was diamond-shaped, I emphasized the motion in Oscar's uplifted wings. I also tilted the photo of the deck, to echo the tilted "Oscar" mat. Note, too, the mat behind the flower pot is actually a little small, allowing the flowers to blend in with the patterned paper. Before you affix the page elements, experiment with tilting and sizes.

Birdless in St. Louis

I could not find an embellishment of a hummingbird the size or style that I wanted. Then I saw this plastic stencil at the same time I noticed the return address sticker from my grandmother. By using the return address sticker as a color guide, I colored in the stencil. Using water color pencils, I was able to go back over my colored bird and blend the colors so that there were no division lines between the stencil segments. If you start with the lightest colors in your palette, you can always add more as you go. Keep tweaking your work, and you'll wind up with an acceptable piece of adornment.

WRITING: *Highlighting with Bullet Points*

Create a WHO, WHAT, WHEN, WHERE, WHY and HOW sentence about your topic.

❧ *OR* ❧

Begin the process of looking up a topic on the Internet and printing out the information.

Now, who knows if any of this is usable material?

—Anne Lamott

Great question, assuming you are lucky enough to have lots of information to work with. I could have stopped with my introductory journaling sentence: "This is Oscar, the ruby-throated hummingbird, that frequented our porch the Summer of 1998." But I was on the Internet, so I took a few extra minutes to see what I could learn.

Wow. I hit a motherlode of information. What a delight! I learned so much that I decided to print out all four pages and read them through carefully. Then I highlighted the most significant information.

If you are like most of us, you started scrapbooking to preserve your family's memories. I never dreamed that scrapbooking could also offer me a way to learn more about the world around me. Yet, it has. Whenever I do a page, I have the chance to continue my education.

Gathering usable information makes it easier to write. Professional writers often talk about the hassle of "writing around" a topic. You "write around" a topic when you don't have enough information and you must stay within the boundaries of your ignorance. More information means more freedom and more to draw from.

I learned that Oscar's dive-bombing was the macho-machinations of a male hummer who had staked out our feeder as the exclusive property of his harem. We always wondered why some birds were allowed access, and some were "buzzed off." Thanks to my scrapbooking, now we know Oscar was a man with a mission.

BONUS TIP # 5:

Packing labels, instructions and manuals make great additions to your scrapbook pages. We live in an information hungry world, and manufacturers know that. I like to color photocopy this sort of memorabilia for my pages. Sometimes I even soak off the labels on products, put them on wax paper while they're wet, let them dry, and copy them to get authentic lettering styles.

Be Ye Fisherwomen of the 'Net

Nothing but 'Net. I love the Internet. My personal favorite search engine is www.dogpile.com but you will probably find others that work well for you. As much as I love the 'Net, as a journalist, I need to caution you: Not everything on the Internet is right, fair or accurate. Remember, anyone can post information online. Those of us trained in journalism school know the "three sources" rule. That is, unless I have three sources for the same data, I can't assume it has a reasonable chance of being accurate. When you find information, look carefully at its source. Then, proceed with caution.

◄ **Write** down the WHO, WHAT, WHEN, WHERE, WHY and HOW. (Of course, you may not have one of these components, such as the HOW, but strive to answer all of them.) Now combine these to make a lead sentence for your journaling.

Search for a topic on the Internet. ▶ I used www.dogpile.com and the word *hummingbird*. Print out the information that appeals to you. Highlight sentences you may use.

Big & Easy Bullets

For many people, the hardest part of writing is transitions. Moving from one idea to another stumps them. So, if this is tough for you, use bullets. Bullets guide the reader through information without pausing for transitions. You can use asterisks or circles or dots or whatever. Try them!

◄ **Copy** what you want to use onto your computer. Use bullets to separate the new ideas. Select a type size, style and color. Print out a copy on "waste" paper. Check for sizing and accuracy. Print out a good copy on archival quality paper.

Going 'Round in Circles

I started the Oscar's story with one sentence about the bird and his feeder under the page title of his name. I continued in the final bullet to tell what happened to his feeder when it was vandalized by a hungry raccoon. This is called "circular construction." It's circular because of starting and ending with the same topic and is a wonderful way of tying ideas together.

Add Narrative to Bullets for Rich Writing

Jay Amberg and Mark Larson tell us that narrative writing can be defined as "a story, an orderly personal account of an experience or event." By adding the simplest narrative, a lead sentence telling WHO, WHAT, WHEN, WHERE, WHY and HOW, you quickly explain to your reader why this page was important to you.

Note that Amberg and Larson chose the adjective "orderly" to describe how the flow should go. They know that most people plunge into an anecdote any which way. Pity the poor listener or reader. Ever enter a conversation part of the way through and realize you are lost? Be a considerate storyteller. Give your audience the background they need to follow the thread of your tale. By adding a narrative sentence to bullets or pull out quotes, you can pack a lot of wonderful information into a small space.

? STORY STARTERS

*Ever visit a place that
was fantastic beyond
your imagination?
What made it so un-
usual? What unexpect-
ed situations have
brought you excite-
ment or drama?*

A Dream Vacation in Egypt

One Tuesday morning, my husband called from his office. I was in the middle of writing a scrapbooking article. "How would you like to go to Cairo?" he said. I brushed him off, thinking of my looming deadline and the possible vaccinations we'd need. Then I started to think. I had always wanted to go to Egypt. What was I waiting for? I made a few calls to doctors. I did a little research. Turns out, we were good-to-go with the shots we'd already had. On Thursday my 10-year-old son, my husband and I flew to Cairo. It was more fascinating and spectacular than I ever dreamed.

CRAFTING: *Combining Full and Partial Pages*

◄ **Print out** the journaling, leaving a 2 1/4" top margin. Leave spaces for embellishments. Cut a piece of patterned paper 2" wide. Run a line of HERMAfix on the back of a solid paper near the edge. Trim a piece of solid paper 1/3" wide. Affix the patterned strip of paper to the top of the page. Add the strip of solid paper to the bottom of the patterned paper.

Cut three triangles out of paper that compliments the solid paper. Arrange and affix the triangles to represent the pyramids. Journal on and trim papers to 9" so that the borders show across the top of all the pages. ▶

◄ **Slip** ticket stubs or other embellishments into an archival pocket and adhere them to the page. Affix the photos to the pages. Color in blank letter stickers and add headlines to the pages.

Tip!

The Short and the Long of It

Page titles are time-consuming. When you have a lot of material to save, like I did from our Egypt trip, why not make one nifty title that tops all your work? This page title runs 2" deep and across the inside of the 8 1/2" x 11" first and last pages. But the interior pages are cut shorter so that the page title shows above these partial pages (8 1/2" x 9") as I added them to the center of my album.

Tip!

Pack Plenty of Film

Always carry more film than you need. Buying film can be a real pain. In Egypt and in England, the price was nearly two times what I normally pay. I won't even discuss the price of film at amusement parks. When I'm not sure where I'll be taking photos, I load my camera with Kodak Max 400 ASA film, the most versatile film in their line.

Memorabilia—It's the Real Thing, Baby

Adding memorabilia to your pages can be tricky. Often the items you save are loaded with acid. But, with a little prudence, you can add the "real thing" to your pages. The result? Authenticity and texture that's unsurpassed. Here's how:

1) Slip the items into archival pockets such as the ones from 3L.

2) Use de-acidify spray for paper items with a special spray such as Archival Mist.

3) Create a pocket from an archival page protector. (You can sew the edges together or use double-sided tape to close it up.)

WRITING: *Stashing and Saving, Then Borrowing*

I begin a new project by assigning it a manila folder, and as I come across relevant material, I put it in the folder.
—Eugene Griessman

Griessman is not alone. Many writers use the file folder technique to gather information as they write. The folders keep information organized and easy to retrieve.

Scrapbookers can use the same technique. Although tips for organizing supplies abound, few mentions are made of how to organize reference material intended for later use.

First, you need to know what to look for. I make it a habit to grab any free pieces of promotional material I can. Often these pieces are written by terrific writers who know how to pack interesting information into small spaces. Brochures, pamphlets, sales literature, advertisements, marketing pieces, point of purchase display material, and postcards all come home with me. When I travel, I bring a Tyvek envelope along and pop all my goodies inside. After I get home, I sort everything and purge duplicates.

More and more hotel properties offer postcards and promotional literature free to guests. Look inside the folder with a room service menu or a list of guest services.

The more information you have, the easier it is to write. Don't worry about lifting whole phrases. Your scrapbook is begging for this information. This isn't sixth grade and you won't be punished for plagiarism. Adding fulsome descriptions to your skimpy handwritten notes will fill in your remembrances.

Elaborate on your photos, as well. Although you can see the filagree arches at the front of our hotel, I couldn't get a uniformed doorman in the picture, so I described him. As you cull your photos, use the discard pile to help you remember pertinent details before you give the blurry or redundant snapshots the heave ho.

> Underline or highlight information from a brochure that you'd like to use in your journaling.
>
> ❧ *OR* ❧
>
> Begin the process of looking up a topic on the Internet and printing out information.

A Guest is a Gift of God: Moslem Proverb

Every traveler must first make peace with fear... then tackle the natives. When Debbie Mock, editor of *Memory Makers* magazine, traveled to Spain, she made a page and put two words on it: *Fear* and *Courage*. Often we neglect to write about the most important part of life, the emotions it engenders. Were you worried about your travels? Were you thrilled and filled with elation? The Egyptian guide books frightened me. I worried for my child's safety, and for my own safety as a non-Moslem woman in a Moslem country. Now, I can look back and laugh! My son was treated like visiting royalty, and I was accepted as what I am, an American woman eager and interested to learn about another culture and religion.

Photocopy your literature. Designate a variety of colored highlighters so that each color stands for a different topic. For example, highlight all information about lodgings in yellow, all information about traveling companions in pink, and so on.

What to Save

When traveling, save:

- Ticket stubs
- Coins and paper money
- Newspaper articles
- Brochures
- Travel manifests
- Receipts
- Programs
- Postcards
- Stationery
- TV Guides

Number all the highlighted lines. Type them into your computer in order.

Edit what you write. Add transitions. Set the margins. Print out a rough draft and check it for sizing. Make adjustments as needed.

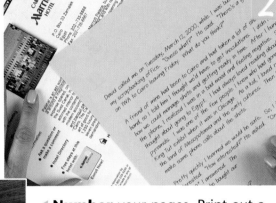

Number your pages. Print out a final draft on archival paper. Add photos to your pages.

Coloring Letter Stickers

Finding the right color of letter stickers to match the rest of your page can be difficult. Color It Yourself stickers give you the option of using markers to get the color just right. Since the letter stickers are glossy, give your ink a while to dry after you color them in with markers. As a bonus, they come in a variety of type styles and sizes. On these pages, using two sizes worked to give emphasis to the important word, EGYPT.

Working with Children to Save Memories

Michael's teacher and I colluded on his homework for this trip. She assigned him the task of creating a scrapbook about his trip. He wrote a few notes every day. Then on our return, we sat down and went over what had happened on a daily basis. Michael looked over the photos and decided which ones he wanted to use. We typed a draft into the computer and printed it out on archival paper, leaving room for the photos he had selected. Together, we mounted the photos on the pages, created a title page, and put the scrapbook into a binder. When we finished, Michael made a presentation to both the 5th and 6th grade classes. That evening, when Michael returned home with his notebook, he gave it a proprietary pat and said, "Now I can keep this and remember my trip for the rest of my life."

Kiawah Island Glossary

American Alligators--Roam the island. Average size between 6 and 8 feet. Look like logs in the water. Like to sunbathe on grassy banks to maintain body temperature.

Angel Oak--Oldest living thing east of the Mississippi, estimated at 1400 years old. Height is 65 feet and circumference is 25.5 feet. The canopy presents the aura of an angel, but the tree is a live oak named for previous owners.

Ashley-Cooper River--The two rivers that conjoin to form the peninsula on which Charleston stands. Their waters flow into the Charleston Harbor.

Barrier Island--An island that holds the sea away from the land, may be bounded on one side with fresh water. Because of its unique position, such an island is home to a wide variety of plants and animals.

The Battery--(Official name is White Point Gardens)--The landscaped park on the tip of the peninsula that is Charleston. The view from the park is toward Fort Sumter.

Beachwalker Park--A public park on Kiawah with a wide, sandy beach. Best place we know for crabbing...

Bene Wafers--Sesame seed cookies that taste a bit like peanut brittle. The Africans who came to the Carolinas brought sesame (or bene seed) and baked these cookies for good luck.

Blackbeard--(Edward Teach)--The notorious pirate who was captured and held in the Charleston Dungeon.

Blockade Runners--Private entrepreneurs who defied the blockade imposed by Lincoln to cut the South off from commerce.

Blue Crabs--Gourmet eating! These crabs require both inshore brackish waters and high salinity ocean waters to complete their life cycles.

? STORY STARTERS

What special vocabularies do you have? Do you have "code words" for family problems or jokes? Do you use jargon at work?

TOOLBOX

SUPPLIES USED

Paper:	Memories Forever
Stamp:	Scrapbookin' Stamps for Journaling
Ink:	Ink jet printer; ColorBox
Pens:	Avery; Sakura Micron
Pencils:	Watercolour pencils by Derwent

A Language All Our Own

A business acquaintance and I were chatting on the phone when he mentioned he would not be in the office the next week. He was off to Kiawah. "Kiawah?" I yelped. "Angel Oak, Beachwalker, Blue Crabs..." and in a matter of seconds we were sharing a language known only to those who love this barrier island off the coast of South Carolina. After I put down the phone, I reflected on the importance of vocabulary. The right word evokes such an impeccable image. Out of that musing came the idea for this glossary page, one of many in my Kiawah album.

CRAFTING: *Creating a Collage Page*

◄ **Stamp** the sand and critter stamp across a piece of beige paper, repeating the pattern from left to right. Use a pen to add dots, extending the ridges of sand and filling in the areas between the stamped images. Color with markers and pencils. Cut along the top of the sand.

Trace the crab on the opposite ► page or draw it freehand. Color it in and label it. Trim around the outside. Trace a map of the Charleston area. Label it. Trim it. Cut out around the silhouette of the Angel Oak and the Angel Oak label.

◄ **Trace** the alligator from the opposite page. Design transfer (see box on page 59) the alligator and cut it out. Tear the light blue paper and tear the darker blue paper. Dot it with white ink and arrange it in rows behind the sand. Affix all of the elements to the page.

A Collage is a Crazy Quilt of Images

A collage offers a terrific way to show a variety of images on one page. Here silhouettes are combined with a postcard and line drawings. The torn paper contrasts with the dotted images on the sand. When making your collage, realize that the more textures you use, the more interesting the scene will be. Play with elements, overlapping a few and letting others cover their neighbors.

You can also use a collage when you have lots of photos of one event, scene or activity. The irregularity of the collage makes similar images dynamic and dramatic.

Scrapbookin' Stamps

Scrapbookin' Stamps for Journaling (shown in box #1) create wonderful lines for your journaling. But, they also make interesting images like the dunes for this beach scene. To join several stamped images together, I used a Micron fine point pen and added dots.

Mark It Up!

Archival markers excel in versatility. Use them to:

• Color in letters on page titles.

• Shade images as shown with the sand dunes here.

• Color in images as done here on vellum with the map of Charleston.

• Use white markers dabbed on with a sponge to create the clouds and the foam on the waves.

• Color in the stamp dies with markers. You can use several colors in a small space with the markers' tiny tips.

WRITING: *Developing a Glossary*

Highlight glossary words in the information you've collected about a topic.

❧ OR ❧

Create definitions for your glossary words.

The commonest [writer's] tool of all, the bread of writing, is vocabulary.
—Steven King

In the beginning was the Word, and oh, what a difference the right word makes. To find the exact word, that perfect word, makes a writer's heart strings zing.

Although by strict definition, glossary words are difficult or specialized, in your glossary the words can simply be ones which are meaningful to you. Here's how:

1) **Begin** by looking at photos and items pertaining to your glossary topic. (The visual cues will help your creative juices simmer.)

2) **Brainstorm** to bring related words to mind. If possible, brainstorm with a friend who is knowledgeable about your topic.

3) **Write** the words down as quickly as possible without censoring yourself. Don't worry about spelling or exact phrasing.

4) **Turn** to any literature you have about your topic and copy down any glossary words that appeal to you.

5) **Need** more help? Flip through a phone directory's yellow pages, and then attack your glossary words by category as listed in the phone book.

6) **Need** more help? Go to the Internet and look up your topic. Print out what you find. Highlight possible glossary words.

Don't forget, since this is your glossary, you can "fudge" a bit by adding proper names, names of places and code words your family uses. (As an example, one child calls Disneyland DeeDah Land. So, add DeeDah Land as one of your glossary entries.)

Now, define your words and add them to your scrapbooking page. On the Kiawah page, I put the words in alphabetical order, but you could also group words by topics.

Build Your Stockpile of Raw Writing Materials

As you go about your daily life, collect information for later use in your journaling. A catalog might share the background of a favorite greeting card designer. A magazine article might tell you how that flower you planted got its name. An interview from the newspaper might share the best explanation you've ever seen for how a solar eclipse happens. Toss your tidbits into a resource file for later use. When you have background information, you don't need to start from scratch as a writer. That blank screen or blank sheet of paper is what causes so much of what we call "writer's block."

Gather all the information you have about a topic. Begin a list of words specific to the topic you've chosen. Add to this list by brainstorming other words.

Start to define your glossary words. Don't worry about giving an approved academic definition. Simply use your own words to explain your glossary.

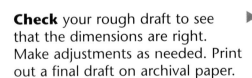

Type your glossary into your computer, alphabetizing the words as you go. Then add definitions. Arrange the words and definitions in columns. Print out a rough draft.

Check your rough draft to see that the dimensions are right. Make adjustments as needed. Print out a final draft on archival paper.

BONUS TIP #6:

Get your money's worth from your rubber stamps. Look carefully at the photo of the rubber stamp on the top of page 35. The lines of sand were created for you to write on. Now look again and get creative. Besides journaling, you could use the stamp for a background of beach as I did, or you could only ink the starfish and sea shell and print them as embellishments. If you ink the lines but not the starfish and sea shell, you could use the stamp to create ridges of snow. The questions to ask are, "What is this like?" and "What could this be?"

Thrifty Tip Alert

I hate wasting good paper, so I always print out my rough draft on non-archival paper. Since this paper is usually thinner than my good paper, it's easy to hold my rough print and my layout up to the light and see where I need to make adjustments in sizing. Because I type up several journaling boxes at once, I can get several journaling boxes on one sheet of good paper.

Visual Impact

Making a narrow column of the glossary gives you a simple but striking page layout. The glossary forms the outside left and right borders. The visual images go inside the borders. You could use this format to make an entire album of a vacation place, a travel adventure, or a special event.

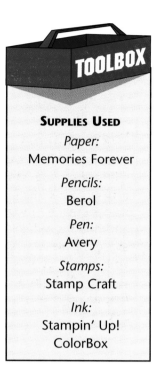

TOOLBOX

SUPPLIES USED

Paper:
Memories Forever

Pencils:
Berol

Pen:
Avery

Stamps:
Stamp Craft

Ink:
Stampin' Up!
ColorBox

STORY STARTERS

What caused giggles in your crowd lately? When was the last time you had a good laugh? Who did something entirely unexpected?

BONUS TIP #7:

Create a "morgue" of images to use on your pages. A "morgue" is an old newspaper term for a collection of information or images to be used some time in the future. Get an accordion file and add four or five folders labeled with general categories like animals, things, people, titles, and scenes. When you find a graphic you like in print media, rip it out and toss it in. My little crab waited in my morgue for months 'til I used him.

The Question of the Day Is...

At the 2000 Great American Scrapbook Show, scrapbooker Nancy Wagner showed me a great idea. While she was on a trip to England, Nancy asked her travel partners a "question of the day." The question became one of the journaling points in her England album. I used the same technique later that summer. When the boys and I were sitting in the car either waiting or driving, the following questions were real life-savers. What was your favorite activity today? All week? What was your least favorite? This page came directly from my notes on the boys' replies.

CRAFTING: *Stamping Directly on Your Page*

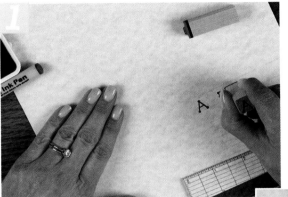

Use the Journaling Genie Vanishing Ink Pen (VIP) to draw three lines in the lower right corner of the two pages. Stamp on your headline using the VIP lines to keep your letters straight. Repeat the process to make your left page title. Draw two lines on the left side of your two page spread.

Use a VIP pen to create more lines under the right page title for journaling. (The page title should be dry by now so the ink doesn't smear.) Journal first with the VIP pen, then with an archival pen.

Affix your photos to the page. Journal cutlines below the photos. Add the crab and dab ink behind him to look like water. Wrap string around a paper stick. Glue the string and stick it to the left page, extend the string across and glue it down on the right page with the crab.

Create Cute Cutlines

The journalism term for the words directly below a photo is "cutline." Of all the areas on a page, this space will enjoy high readership, so take advantage of this space.

Tilt!

Tipping your photos allows you to "crop" pictures without ever handling a pair of scissors. Here I judiciously covered my backside. Ahem. Before you affix your pics to the page, play with your angles to see what looks good. Tilted photos add a zippy feel to the pages and give an illusion of motion.

Texture Tales

Add texture to pages with string, jute, embroidery floss, dental floss, wire, net, mesh and ribbons. Whenever possible, check with manufacturers to see if their products are archivally safe.

Stamp a Title

The rubber stamps on this page are perfect for inking a page title. The size makes them versatile and the style goes with everything. If you haven't tried stamping on your pages, you might want to start with an alphabet set. First, stamp the letters onto a separate paper until you are fairly confident of your abilities. Then, try your hand at stamping directly onto the paper. The stamps make headings fun, easy and fast.

WRITING: *Taking Notes and Asking Questions*

Your notebook, remember, is your repository for everything—from research notes to quotes to observations made on the fly.

—David Fryxell

Write down the questions you might like to ask others during your vacation.

⁂ *AND* ⁂

Recopy answers to your questions on a scrapbooking page.

Taking notes ranks right up there as the easiest and simplest way to improve your writing. Invest in two or three notebooks small enough to carry in your pocket, your purse and the glove compartment of your car. Train yourself to jot down a word or two on the spot. You can always go back and fill in the rest of your musings.

If you are traveling with a group, ask daily questions as prompts to get the crowd talking. You might want to ask the following:

❏ What is the most fascinating sight you've had on this trip?

❏ What was the best meal? What was the worst meal?

❏ What was better than you expected? What was worse?

❏ What was the funniest moment on our trip?

❏ What was your favorite activity? What did you like the least?

❏ What made you think? What caused you to want to learn more?

❏ What is it you can't wait to share with someone back home?

❏ What was the best part of the trip? What was the worst part?

❏ What would you like to see again?

❏ What do you wish you had brought? What should you have left at home?

❏ Who do you wish was here to share this with you? Why?

❏ What changes might you make in your life as a result of this adventure?

If you ask these questions daily, you'll get different responses as the trip progresses. The boys and I had fun reviewing what we'd seen and done at the close of each day. I think you will, too.

Accentuate the Positive

I can't overemphasize the importance of teaching kids to review the day and conclude their thoughts with a positive focus. No matter what went wrong, we can always be thankful. So often, we put our heads on the pillow only to worry about the next day. Making positive focus a habit keeps us on the right track psychologically and spiritually. When we get down in the dumps, we play a game of naming "one good thing." Each family member must find "one good thing," and we all take turns. Soon, we are competing to name all the happy stuff we were so willing to cast aside.

Designate a notebook for travel memos. Put your name and address inside in case you and the notebook are separated. With each entry, include the date and your destination. Make entries daily if possible. Keep receipts to help you track where you visit and where you eat. Add dates and information from receipts to your notebook.

Type the information into the computer. Use a spell-checker to make sure your spelling is correct, and a grammar program to flag you on any big grammatical errors. Rewrite as necessary.

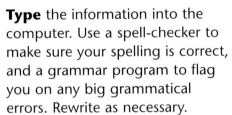

Use a VIP pen to draw lines for journaling. Copy the computer copy by hand with an archival pen onto the archival scrapbook page.

Punch It Up!

If you only have the time to write a few words, capture the punch line, the words that set up the rest of the story. Then you can go back and fill in information at your leisure.

Bag 'Em, Danno

Debbie Mock, editor of *Memory Makers* magazine, brings plastic baggies along with her when she travels. At the end of each day, Debbie sorts her memorabilia and receipts. This makes it easier for her to track where she went and what she did. Keeping track of where you were and when you were there gets very complicated when you cross a dateline. You either lose a day or gain a day, and I've found that figuring out what happened when is harder than I would have guessed.

Making An Album, One Page at a Time

Notice the similarities between these pages and the ones on pages 34 and 38? To create visual continuity in an album, you can:

1) **Use** the same background paper. I used the Memories Forever blue-toned paper because it went with so many of the beach scenes.

2) **Keep** paper in the same style or color family. For example, Keeping Memories Alive has a line called the Cottage Collection. Although the papers are different colors and patterns, they create the same mood.

3) **Use** background paper from one manufacturer. The Ever After line of paper has similar weight and style. You could alternate colors within the Ever After line and still maintain a consistent feel.

4) **Stay** with a core "wardrobe" of paper colors, but alternate these throughout your album. For a remembrance album honoring my grandmother, I used cream, olive green, peachy orange, and a floral. These colors mimicked the colors in my grandmother's home.

? STORY STARTERS

Which "old friends" have you stayed in touch with? How did you meet? What experiences from your years in high school still have meaning for you?

TOOLBOX

SUPPLIES USED

Paper:	Solid black and red by Memories Forever
Font:	Times Roman
Stickers:	Dot Tip Alphabet by Fresh & Funky
Pens:	Avery; Zig
Other:	Archival Mist; Color photocopier

The Odd Couple is an Odd Trio After All These Years

Almost 30 years ago, eight of us students at Griffith High School appeared in a student production of The Odd Couple. Three of us have gotten back in contact with each other in the past few years. When I came across the clipping from our school paper and a press photo, I wondered what the guys remembered from our experience. I wanted to create a page that included all of our thoughts from our diverse life styles, but showing our similar tastes. So, I sent an e-mail to Bill and Doug. They responded promptly. The result was unforgettable and made a poignant page.

CRAFTING: *Color Copying Your Embellishments*

◄ **Color photocopy** six playing cards at 100% so that each individual card shows. Arrange the cards in a line overlapping each other as shown on the page. Color photocopy them at 20%. Make several copies. Trim the line of cards and tape them together on the back to form a border.

Color in uncolored letter stickers ► to match the colors of the playing cards. Let them dry, then arrange the letters on the page to create a headline. (As you can see, you'll get a lot of titles from one sheet of stickers.)

◄ **Mat** a photo with white and then colored paper. Spray the article with de-acidifying spray, then mat it. Print and mat journaling boxes. Affix all the elements to the pages.

Journaling is a Graphic Element for Pages

Once in a while, a scrapbooker will tell me that she doesn't add journaling because she doesn't like the way it looks on her page. That doesn't make sense. We are more accustomed to seeing pages with lots of type and fewer photos than pages filled with photos. Imagine these pages without the journaling. Pretty dull, eh?

If you don't like your handwriting, print your journaling using a computer as I have done here, but for goodness sake, don't leave out journaling to make your pages prettier. Play with different print sizes and styles. Leave wide white borders around your journaling blocks. Mat the journaling blocks. Break up large areas of type into smaller boxes. But don't leave out the story!

Tip!

Mat Journaling Boxes for Impact

This is so important that I'll repeat myself: Mat your journaling boxes for impact. Treat them like any other graphic element on the page, and you'll learn to love the look of pages that include journaling.

Tip!

But Can You Read It?

Different fonts convey different feelings. This type is sans serif and has a clean, bold look to it. Serif type (remember? with the shoulders on the letters?) looks more formal and is easier to read. Don't use fancy scrapbook fonts for large areas of journaling. While these specialty fonts are perfect for page titles, when grouped in paragraphs they are hard to read. Before you print out your journaling on archival paper, try several typefaces. One is sure to give you the look and feel you want.

WRITING: *Start a Dialogue*

Dialogue gives the reader the guilty pleasure of being a fly on the wall.
—Tam Mossman

Well said. We all love to read dialogue that's lively and entertaining. What could be more fun than reading dialogue about a topic near and dear to our hearts?

Of all the pages I've done for this book, The Odd Couple pages surprised me the most. I never knew how worried Doug was. Or how proud Bill felt. Of course, initially I felt hesitant asking them to add to my book on scrapbooking, but now that I have their responses, I'm very thankful.

You'll get the best response to a request for dialogue if you start by sharing your own thoughts. First, your written information instructs your dialogue pals in what to do. Second, your written information sets the mood for their shared comments. You may need to edit responses slightly because your correspondents won't know how much space you have. Still, if my experience is any guide, you'll be thrilled with what you receive.

Who might you dialogue with?

1) **Siblings**—to garner their memories of shared events, places or people.

2) **School mates**—to glimpse how they saw you and the time you spent together.

3) **Peers**—to share how all of you felt about a significant time in your lives. One scrapbooker wrote me that she doesn't have children, so she felt like she didn't have much to scrap. Then she opened a dialogue with peers of her age about growing up during the Cuban Missile Crisis. The result was fascinating and gave her an entire album of reminiscences about the times of her life.

4) **Friends**—to get their impressions of newsworthy events or adventures you've shared.

And the list goes on and on.

> Draft a request for information from other people whose input you'd like to add to a scrapbooking page.
> *AND*
> Edit the responses.

If Both of You Agree, One of You is Unnecessary

In the long hot summers of my girlhood, my sister and I would trade 50¢ and pop bottle caps for the air-conditioned comfort of the afternoon movies. Jane and I look alike, but we are very different people. One evening after a movie, my mom called us into the kitchen. "You both told me about the movie you watched and your versions were so different that I want to know..." she paused. "Did you go to the same show?" Yes, we had. But sitting there and hearing Jane tell her re-hash of the movie shocked me, too. Where did she get that stuff? She sat beside me for two hours, but her focus and mine drifted off to separate scenes.

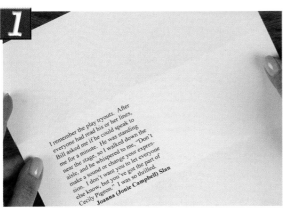

Write your portion of the dialogue. Focus on your memories of the event. Make copies.

Share your written piece with your dialogue participants. Ask them to write down their memories.

Type their responses into the computer. Edit all the comments. Put all the comments into the same format. Print out a rough copy.

Refine the print copy. Check the margins and adjust them if necessary. Print onto archival paper. Trim and add the journaling to the page.

Take the Lead and Move Out Ahead

Author and editor David Fryxell tells writers that good leads "telegraph to the reader what's to come, so he or she can make an informed decision of whether to read on." Of all the sentences you write in your journaling or in your correspondence, the first, or *lead*, sentence is the most important. A good lead quickly convinces the readers to pay attention. When I sent an e-mail to my Odd Couple friends, I wrote: Calling Oscar and Felix—I need help—Cecily Pigeon.

Immediately, the guys focused on my e-mail from the line-up of mail they received that date. Think: Attention–Request–Rationale. I got their attention by using their stage names, the request came by asking for help, and the rationale was clear: I reminded them by using my character name from a special time we shared.

Touching Others

This journaling idea touches the emotions in a way you'll cherish. Often we go through life and never tell people what they've meant to us, but a dialogue page gives us the chance to say, "I'm so glad my life and yours intersected. You made a difference to me." With this type of page, our scrapbook becomes a way to touch others as we preserve tender memories for ourselves.

TOOLBOX

SUPPLIES USED

Paper:
Memories Forever

Stars/Barn Red by
Paperabilities III

Punches:
Family Treasures

Stamps:
Clear Stamps

Ink:
Archival Inks by
Ranger Industries

Pens:
Berol

Other Supplies:
Archival Mist

? STORY STARTERS

*How do other adults
see your child? What
are your child's strong
points?*

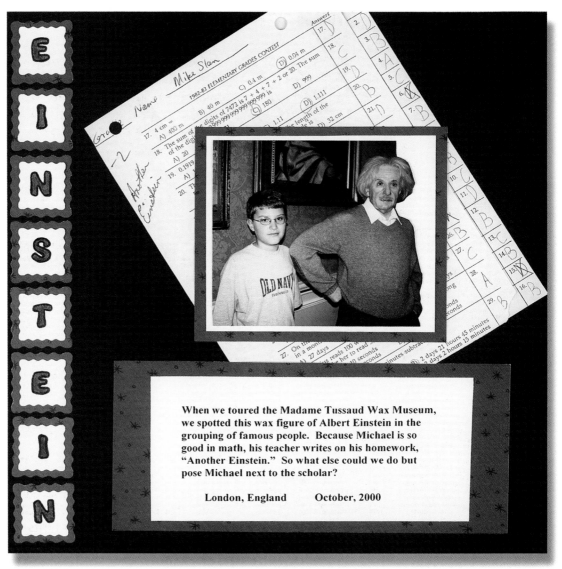

When we toured the Madame Tussaud Wax Museum,
we spotted this wax figure of Albert Einstein in the
grouping of famous people. Because Michael is so
good in math, his teacher writes on his homework,
"Another Einstein." So what else could we do but
pose Michael next to the scholar?

London, England   October, 2000

Another Einstein

When we saw "Einstein" at Madame Tussauds Wax Museum, I instantly remembered Michael's math teacher's comment on his homework. Although my family complains that I'm a pack rat, holding on to class assignments and teacher's notes really pays off. Adding memorabilia like this strengthens your page because you are including a real artifact rather than simply telling a story. Plus, the portrait of my son is strengthened by sharing the viewpoint of another person, his teacher.

CRAFTING: *Saving and Adding Memorabilia*

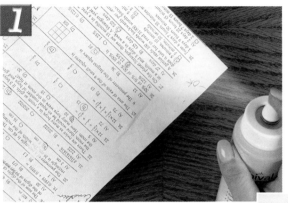

◀ **Determine** whether the memorabilia you have will fit on the page. If so, spray them with de-acidifying spray to make them safe. Let them dry. Crop the memorabilia as needed.

Punch out small tile lettering boxes. Put HERMAfix on the back of the tiles and secure them to a waste piece of paper. Stamp the letters onto the tiles, taking care to center them. Color in the letters. ▶

◀ **Punch out** the larger tiles. Affix the small tiles within the larger tiles. Apply HERMAfix to the back of the double tiled letters. Mat the photo. Affix all of the elements to the page.

Totally Tile

Tile lettering makes great looking headlines like this. Now that Family Treasures has tile punches in incremental sizes, these tiles are easier than ever to make.

Acid Free for a Fee

Wow. The price on a can of de-acidifying spray will knock your socks off. BUT...it's well worth the investment. You can use it to make all sorts of memorabilia safe for inclusion on your pages. If you don't want to pop for the spray, you could make color copies of the stuff. But that has a cost to it also. And, copies don't have the same texture that originals have. So splurge on the spray.

Save Notes from EVERYBODY...

Notes are so telling! Consider all these subtleties: What is the note written on? What was it written in—ink, pencil or crayon? What color ink was used? Did the person write or print? How was it signed? Was the note written neatly in a margin or scrawled across other material?

Be an amateur psychologist. The next time you receive a note look for clues to the writer's personality.

WRITING: *Asking When, Then, Why and So What?*

Write down an explanation of a nickname, phrase or comment.

❧ *OR* ❧

Spray memorabilia with Archival Mist and let it dry.

Looking back, I imagine I was always writing. Twaddle it was too. But better far write twaddle or anything, anything, than nothing at all.

—Katherine Mansfield

Getting started is the toughest part of writing. We worry that we have nothing to say. That's why the "When, Then, Why and So What" formula works so well. All you need to do is fill in the blanks.

For this page, the WHEN was "When we toured Madame Tussaud's Wax Museum. The THEN is a shorthand form of "Then we did what?" In this case the THEN becomes "We spotted this wax figure of Albert Einstein in the grouping of famous people." Now the WHY gives an explanation of what happened next. So, our WHY says "Because Michael is so good in math, his teacher writes on his homework, *Another Einstein.*"

Finally, the SO WHAT? gives the reader the conclusion or the resolution of the situation. For us, with the proximity of Einstein and knowledge of our son's nickname, SO WHAT? else could we do but pose Michael next to the scholar. Since the replica of the genius looks so real, we had an unusual photograph to take back to the math teacher.

Notice how the key words lead you through the writing. All you need to do is fill in the blanks. Of course, you'll want to add the date and the place to your page, but that doesn't have to be included in the journaling box.

Keep a copy of this simple writing map on an index card near where you journal. On those days when you get stuck, use these prompts to haul you back into the driving lane.

One reason these cues work so well is their sound background in the dramatic arts. Most drama is built on a simple formula: background, action, climax and resolution. We've rearranged the elements to make your conclusion a bit more zingy. In this case, WHEN is the background. THEN is the action. SO WHAT? is the climax. WHY is the resolution.

Spell Checks Can Bounce, A Cautionary Tale

Spell check is a wonderful invention, but it has its limits. The spellchecker can only tell you a word is spelled correctly if the word exists in its dictionary and if you've used the right word. If I type in "write" and I mean "correct" which would be "right," I'm sunk.

Take your spellchecker with a grain of salt, but do allow it to wave a red flag that alerts you to the possibility you've made a mistake. Recently, I looked up a word in the dictionary that my spellchecker had flagged as wrong. Guess what? The spellchecker version was incorrect, and I was right. When in doubt, get a second opinion.

Copy the questions from this form or download the form from www.scrapbookstorytelling.com (it is under the "Templates" section). Write in the phrases that correspond to your situation.

Type the phrases into the computer. Set the margins to correspond with the journaling box, minus 1/2" on each side. Check the spelling.

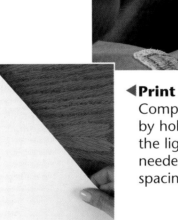

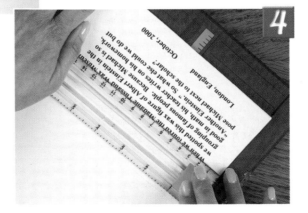

Print out your journaling. Compare it to the journaling box by holding the two papers up to the light. Adjust the margins as needed. Print out and check the spacing again as needed.

Print a final copy of your journaling on archivally-safe paper. Trim the journaling to fit inside the journaling box.

Thicken the Soup

Add as many facts as possible to your writing. For example, notice I shared that Einstein was part of a grouping of famous people.

Que Serif, Serif

Serifs are the little arms and legs that appear on type.

For the cleanest look, go sans serif. For a more formal look, serif type is preferred.

A History of Brown's Hotel

1837--James Brown, the valet of Lord Byron, saw the need for a first-rate genteel inn or hotel. He acquired the leave of 23 Dover Street.

Brown married Lady Byron's personal maid, Sarah Wills. Wills was an astute business woman with high standards of service and great attention to detail.

1851--The 1851 Exhibition put Brown's on the map as visitors came from all over the world.

1876--The first successful telephone call in Britain is made from Brown's by Alexander Graham Bell.

Among Brown's illustrious visitors:
* John Pierpoint Morgan
* Napoleon III
* Empress Eugenie
* Theodore Roosevelt
* Cecil Rhodes
* Rudyard Kipling
* Agatha Christie
* Steven King

1998--Joanna Slan and Elaine Floyd, tired and hungry, wander into Brown's. Entranced by the possibility of a REAL British High Tea, they stay and order refreshments.

2000--Joanna Slan demands that her husband David and son Michael accompany her to Brown's for tea. The Slan men are suitably impressed. While initially leery of just having "tea," Michael succumbs to the pleasures of sandwiches, scones, pastries and sweets while displaying wonderful manners.

? STORY STARTERS

What experiences would you like to share with your family? What was their response? Did they share your enthusiasm?

TOOLBOX

SUPPLIES USED

Paper:	Red and blue solids
Fonts:	Times Roman
Stamps:	ME Inc.; © Susan Branch, All Night Media
Ink:	Ink jet printer; Stampin' Up!
Stickers:	Letter stickers by Paper Adventures
Other:	Trimmer by Fiskars

Stopping for a Proper Cuppa at Brown's Hotel

Brown's Hotel ranks among the top three places in London for High Tea. Although my son and husband rolled their eyes, I insisted that we visit Brown's for a "cuppa." My motive? I wanted to see a certain desk. In his book *On Writing*, Steven King said he wrote the book *Misery* sitting at a desk in Brown's where Rudyard Kipling had written and died of a stroke. But when I asked about the desk, the waiter explained the beautiful piece had been moved. Seeing my disappointment, he brought me a two-page history of Brown's. My point? Share your interest. People will give you fascinating tidbits.

CRAFTING: *Running Your Title Down the Side*

◄ **Stamp** a tea pot on a strip of white paper 2" by 9 $^3/4$". Under the tea pot hand print words. Add letter stickers stacked on top of each other vertically on the paper. Mat the white paper on patterned paper. Mat the patterned paper on a solid.

Stamp a teapot, a cup and a teapot on white paper. Color them and cut them out. Mount one on a square of solid paper. Mat journaling boxes. Mat one photo to be your focal point. ▶

◄ **Crop** photos as desired. Arrange all the elements on the page. Affix the elements to the page. Trim any overhanging elements.

Three for Tea is Thrice the Treat

Visually, three embellishments are more pleasing than one. You can lead the eye through a layout by strategically placing the elements. Note how the teapots move from the upper left to the lower right. Above the teapots, three photos overlap, sharing space and leading the eye. Below two of the photos, the three journaling boxes take the eye from left to right. If you have more space, move from three to five, but always aim for uneven numbers of elements because the eye tends to pair up what it sees.

Lay Down Letters

Try running the page title vertically down one side of a page as I did here, leaving the right hand area free for photos and journaling. Or run the title down the left and right edges, leaving the center open for photos. Either layout offers great visual organization.

Colored Letters

When I saw Paper Adventure's letter stickers, I went wild. Finally, there were letter stickers in the colors I use in my scrapbooks. The stickers are thick enough to peel off the backing without ripping. And, Paper Adventures gives me punctuation marks so I don't have to create an apostrophe by cutting up a letter. You'll want an alphabet in every color. (My son has used these to jazz up his school projects. Letter stickers are much neater and easier than hand printing.)

WRITING: *Writing Chronologically*

Whenever I embark on a story…it helps me to remember two things. One is that writing is linear and sequential. I also try to remember that the reader should be given only as much information as he needs and not one word more.

—William Zinsser

Highlight information you'd like to use in your journaling.

❧ *OR* ❧

Write down dates you'll use in your chronological writings.

Without thinking, the majority of us tell stories in a loose, chronological way. The organization makes sense. We think back to what happened first, second and third and away we go.

Organizing your journaling works the same way. However, on the Brown's page, my chronology was extensive because the hotel's history covers nearly 150 years. Notice how easily the information reads when the date is the starting point. Let the date lead the way and transitions between paragraphs aren't necessary.

Note that I added a smidge of fun. In 1998, my friend Elaine and I wandered into Brown's. I copied the same style as my other entries, making my language a bit stiff and formal. Then in the section labeled 2000, I told the story of my family's visit to Brown's.

By listing the treats Michael "succumbed to," I was able to tell readers the goodies that High Tea includes.

When you journal, remember to include your reaction and the reaction of your family. Without your familial input, the pages become impersonal. Here are questions to ponder:

1) **What was our initial reaction?** Notice I said that I "demanded" we go to Brown's. Using a strong verb, I hinted that the guys were not in agreement with my choice.

2) **What happened once you arrived or became engaged in the situation?** (I wrote that "The Slan men were suitably impressed.") If possible, show contrast between your expectations and reality.

4) **Summarize the situation**. Michael thought "tea" meant exactly that, and he was concerned there wouldn't be enough to eat. He learned this was far from true.

What you and yours think is what makes your scrapbook unique and valuable to your family.

Computer Journaling: Save Yourself Time and Hand Cramps

Journaling with a computer allows you to use much smaller type than most of us can handwrite. As a result, you can put much more into a small space. As an example, although this typeface is small, the style and serifs make it very easy to read.

If you are worried about archival safety, use your computer to print out a copy first, then put your printout on a light table and re-copy the information with an archival pen onto archival paper. You may want to save all the journaling you do on a computer. This gives you a backup copy in case your scrapbook meets an untimely demise.

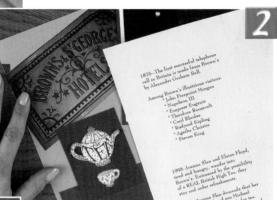

◄ **Photocopy** your information. Highlight information that appeals to you.

Transfer the highlighted information to your computer. Write a title for the top of your journaling. Start each new block of information with a year or date. Double space between blocks of information.

Print out a rough copy of what you've written. Check for spacing. Make adjustments as needed. Leave space so that you can cut the journaling into three blocks. Print onto archival quality paper. ▶

◄ **Cut** the journaling into three copy blocks. Mat it on solid paper. Affix it to the page. Overlap the navy blue block with the tea pot and cup embellishment on the second block. Overlap the teapot embellishment on the third block.

Tip!

Let Pages Steep

At first, these pages only had one teapot at the top of the page title. I kept them out of the album for a couple of days. Then, I realized three teapots would pull the page together and matting the middle pot would help define it. Now I always keep my pages out. They seem to speak to me and tell me what they need.

Tip!

Use Patterns Sparingly

The Pixie Press line of travel paper adds a lively spot of color to all your travel pages. But patterned paper can easily overwhelm your pages. By using patterned paper sparingly as accents, you'll get the feel of the design, you'll stretch your paper further, and you'll keep the focus on your photos. Note, too, dark photos, often do best on lighter backgrounds. The lighter background brightens the page.

Is That Your Final Answer?

To learn more about any topic, ask the next question. Often people stop with one question, especially if they don't sense that their questions are welcomed. When I asked the waiter about Kipling's desk, he dismissed me with, "Oh, that's not here." I hadn't come all the way across an ocean to quit so quickly. As he returned to our table, I continued, "But according to Steven King, the desk is here." Seeing that I was really interested, he paused and smiled, "Yes, well, it was until about five years ago. Why don't I ask for you?" He never did find out exactly where the desk had gone, but he did return with the photocopied information about Brown's. The lesson? Always ask one more question before you give up.

LOVE

1. The wood for Steinway pianos comes from all over the world. Steinway is so particular that they have a wood technologist that selects their wood.
2. It takes over one entire calendar year from the day wood is accepted by the factory until a Steinway is built.
3. The Steinway piano is the choice of 98% of all concert pianists.
4. Steinways as old as 100 years are still used for performance.
5. Steinway has a complete restoration area devoted to rebuilding pianos.
6. There are only 79 Steinway piano dealers in the Americas.
7. In 1999 Steinway re-purchased their 33,000 square foot 57th Street location in Manhattan.
8. Steinway has been the choice of legendary pianists including Horowitz, Rubenstein, and Cliburn.
9. Steinway pianos sound different from all other pianos. The tones are thick and powerful without distortion.
10. Henry Z. Steinway was the former President of Steinway & Sons and now serves as a consultant to the company.

LORE

1. Steinway rims are made of one piece of laminated hard maple that is bent into shape.
2. Steinway has been building pianos since 1853.
3. The Steinway factory is located in Queens, Long Island City, New York.
4. Steinway holds more patents on pianos than any other manufacturer.
5. Steinway actions are fitted for each individual piano. An action from one piano will not fit any other Steinway.
6. Steinway has books dating back to its beginning that record every piano built, its serial number on the plate and the name of the owner.
7. These books are still used today to look up original ownership and "birth dates" of Steinway pianos.
8. Frank Mazurco, Executive Vice President of Steinway, was our district manager before being promoted to New York.
9. In the Steinway factory, visitors must wear safety glasses at all times.
10. There were more Steinway pianos sold in 2000 than in any year since 1926.

? STORY STARTERS

What is your area of expertise? What do you know inside-out? Is there a product or a process that fascinates you or your family?

SUPPLIES USED

Paper:	Making Memories
	Metallic paper by Hygloss
Font:	Times Roman

The Love and Lore of Steinway

My husband has been selling Steinway pianos now for 19 years. But my son and I managed to go on a factory tour of Steinway only recently. When I looked at the pictures I took in the factory, they seemed too mechanical. The warmth I feel toward the company and its people was missing. Then I remembered this photo of Henry Z. Steinway, the last Steinway family member actively involved in the business. Seeing Henry's smile made me smile, remembering all the times he's visited our stores and all the good times we've shared with him at Steinway functions.

CRAFTING: *Combining a Collage and a Primary Focus*

Turn your two pages over and tape them together on the back side using archival tape. Now turn back to the right side of your work. Crop and mat the primary focus photo. Crop the other photos as needed or desired.

Measure 6 ¹/₂" across the bottom of a 12" x 12" piece of contrasting solid paper. Create a right angle triangle by drawing a line from that spot 6 ¹/₂" out to the upper left corner. Cut it. Repeat on another paper, drawing a line from 6 ¹/₂" out to the upper right corner.

Focus with a Photo

Choose a primary focus photo for your work and give that picture special attention. Double or triple mat the photo and give it a prominent place on the page. You may also wish to enlarge your focus photo to give it more power. The Kodak Picture Maker makes enlarging originals easy and economical.

Use HERMAfix to tack down all the background photos. Create a collage. On top of the collage, tack down the primary focus photo. Put right angle triangles in the left and right corners. Add journaling boxes. Turn over the page to the back side and cut the two pages apart.

Photo Collage

Create a photo collage by overlapping a variety of pictures of the same topic. This works particularly well when you want to share a diverse selection of visuals on the same topic. Once you've made your collage, remember you'll still need a focal point.

Triangle Triage

The triangular shape of red on each outside edge narrows the focus so that the center of the page demands your attention. So simple, but so effective.

Tips and Tricks with Color

The bronze of the Steinway name plate is repeated in the mat for the journaling box. The red was taken from the red felt used inside the piano, and the black and white came from the keys. By keeping a simple color palette, you can make your pages more effective and dramatic.

Note, too, that the photo of Henry Z. was matted first in white, then in red. A thin mat of white around a photo adds a crisp look to photos and often makes the second mat even more powerful. So when you're trying to mat a picture and none of the mats look right, try a white inner mat first, then move to a second color.

WRITING: *20 Things About... (Make a List)*

Number your paper from 1 to 20 and start listing points to remember.

AND

Show your list to an expert.

Many experts are easily accessible and will be happy to go over material for you, fill in the missing pieces, and correct mistakes and misconceptions.

—Robert Bly

This technique is both easier and harder than it looks. It's easier because we are accustomed to making lists and, essentially, this is a list. That said, forcing yourself to write 20 things makes you go past the superficial. By the time you hit 15, you're digging, baby. Think of this group of 20 as your own personal rebellion against the obvious journaling that so often shows up on scrapbook pages.

If you get stuck, sleep on this exercise. Yep, your subconscious mind works overtime, so why not let it help you with your scrapbooking? You'll be amazed at what will pop up.

Here's what you do. Review the list before you fall asleep. Keep the list beside your bed. Look at it first thing in the morning. Voila! New thoughts.

No nap in your future? Go for a walk and vigorously swing your arms so that they cross the midline of your body as you walk. Any time you cross your midline, you engage huge portions of your brain. (Think of the calories!)

You can also use 20 Things About... as a warm-up exercise before you write. In fact, fiction writers often create an entire dossier for their made-up characters. Granted, you won't see the dossier published as part of the book, but you'll imagine the character as a three-dimensional person because the writer did her homework. Lists help you get specific.

Still stumped? Think of things from these categories:

- Visual appearance
- Sounds made
- Smells like
- Feels like
- Tastes like

Don't forget to consult an expert. He or she will also help you fill in your list.

Expert Advice—Will Work for Meals

Every family has its experts, and in my house my husband is the guy who knows about pianos. After I typed in my 20 Things About..., I casually asked, "Could you check this over for me?" He plopped right down in front of the computer and immersed himself in his favorite subject. You'll note that I didn't really carefully separate Love and Lore items, per se. I simply liked the size (four letters) and look of the two words as facing headlines for my pages.

Write the numbers 1 to 20 on a sheet of paper. As quickly as possible, write down whatever comes to mind. Add to the list until you come up with 20 items.

Be Specific

Factual information, including specific numbers and proper names, gives credibility to your pages. Whatever your topic, get used to being picky with your words. Later, you'll be glad you did.

Type your list into the computer. ▶ Ask your local expert to scan the list and make suggestions, corrections and additions. Print out the list and adjust the spacing if necessary.

Print out a final version of your list. Trim the list to fit your space. Mat the list and adhere it to the page.

Numero Uno

Simple guidelines for numbers make your journaling more readable.

1. For numbers under 10, write out the word. For numbers 10 and over, use digits.

2. Always write out a number in words if it occurs at the beginning of a sentence.

3. It's not necessary to add a comma when you begin a sentence with a two-word phrase like "In 1999..."

Create a "Cheat Sheet" for Journaling

Too many thoughts buzzing about in your head? Make a list of words or phrases before you start your writing project. This list becomes your raw material inventory. You don't have to use every idea that pops into your mind, but putting those ideas down on paper allows you the freedom to think in a variety of ways and use those words as you see fit.

Ernest Hemingway said, "If a writer stops observing, he is finished. But he does not have to observe consciously nor think how it will be useful." When you sit down to write, you may have information you don't end up using. That's fine. You don't wear every piece of clothing you own all the time do you? Likewise you don't need to parade every bit of information you own either. Be selective.

TOOLBOX

SUPPLIES USED

Paper:
Memories Forever

Font:
Helvetica

Ink:
Laser printer

Lettering:
Chunky white stickers
by Making Memories

Pens:
Avery
Sanford

? STORY STARTERS

What games does your family enjoy playing? What quirks are there in the rules? Who usually wins? How did your family initially hear about their favorite game?

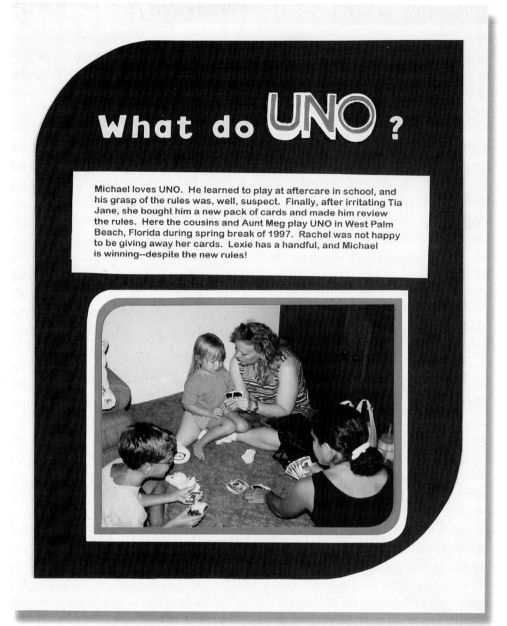

What do UNO?

Michael loves UNO. He learned to play at aftercare in school, and his grasp of the rules was, well, suspect. Finally, after irritating Tia Jane, she bought him a new pack of cards and made him review the rules. Here the cousins and Aunt Meg play UNO in West Palm Beach, Florida during spring break of 1997. Rachel was not happy to be giving away her cards. Lexie has a handful, and Michael is winning--despite the new rules!

What do UNO?

I can't remember when Michael first started playing UNO but I'm always picking up UNO cards around the house. Even so, this is the only picture I have of him playing the game. Best of all, it's a picture of Michael with his cousins. Once I decided to do an UNO page, I was stumped. What exactly do you say about a game? We like to play it? I figured that mindmapping might encourage me to turn up some fascinating tidbit worth writing about. Fortunately, it did. The fact that the cards have such a strong visual design made the page a pleasure to create.

CRAFTING: *Learning Design Transfer Techniques*

◀ **Put** a large curved item such as a jar lid along the upper left corner of your black paper and outline it with a white pencil. Do the same on the lower right corner. Trim it.

Draw the curve with a photo pencil using a smaller curved item on your photo. Trim it. Mat the photo in red and white, trimming the edges as you did for the paper and the photo. Add the journaling box and adhere all the items to the page. ▶

White Pens

You probably know how important black archival pens are to scrapping, but do you realize what you can do with a white pen? On this page, I evened up the inside of the O in UNO with a white pen. You can also use a white pen to correct your journaling mistakes.

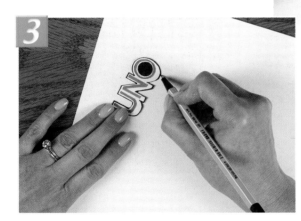

◀ **Create** the words "What do" and the question mark using sticker letters. Rub a pencil on the back of a photocopy of the UNO logo. Flip the photocopy right side up and trace the logo onto a piece of white paper. Fill it in with red marker. Cut out the logo. Color the outside edge of the logo black and adhere it to the black page.

Household Goods Make Good Helpers

Make the most of your scrapbooking dollar by making your household goods do double duty. Use any circular item to outline a circle for cropping. (If you can see through the item, so much the better.) A pizza scraper or the edge of a soft spatula can be slipped under a photo and between photo splits to lift the photo from the page. Or slide a piece of dental floss under the photo to pop it free. (This works especially well to lift photos from old "magnetic" albums.)

Design Transfer Techniques

Remember the good old days and carbon paper? You can make your own version of carbon paper to help you transfer designs to your scrapbook pages. **First**, copy the design to the correct size on a photocopier. **Second**, flip the copy over and color in the back side, especially along the reverse of your design. (You are laying down a layer of carbon that you'll transfer in the next step.) **Third**, trace along the lines of the design on the right side. You'll lay down a faint outline of your design. Now, go over the design with markers or pencils in the colors you want. You can use the same procedure on dark paper by using a white carbon pencil to put the carbon on the back of the image. Erase any unwanted lines when you are done.

WRITING: *Making a Mindmap*

Draw a mindmap, making the center circle and spokes.

≈ *AND* ≈

Start to fill the mindmap in with ideas, words and phrases.

Newly formed ideas are fragile and imperfect—they need time to mature and acquire the detail needed to make them believable.

—James Adam

I suppose he could have noted that a lot of ideas are "half-baked," right? So they're slippery and hard to grasp. Which is why mind-mapping works so well.

Make a circle in the middle of a piece of blank paper. Inside the circle, write down a topic. Without censoring yourself, quickly write the thoughts that come to mind inside new little circles. If you get another thought about that first thought, attach it to your bubble with a line.

Don't get hung up about what your mindmap looks like. What is important is generating ideas in an unrestricted way. Eventually, you'll get so that you cluster like ideas together. That makes for better organization, and thus for easier writing. However, in the beginning, your goal is simply to generate topic-related ideas as fast as possible in a non-linear formation.

You might be wondering, "Why not outline my topic?" Outlining is linear and sequential. Perhaps you've had the experience of making an outline then looking back and discovering that you have information that didn't fit anywhere. It happens.

Most of us remember in non-linear ways. Inside our brain are links that seem nonsensical. If you force yourself into a linear format for remembering, you'll evade that portion of your brain with the "good stuff."

Joyce Wycoff says in her book *Mindmapping*, "By allowing us to freely interact with information, and by adding color, symbols and organization to the information as we receive it, mindmapping helps us develop the full potential of our minds. We develop better memories, more powerful organizational skills and more creativity."

Once you master mind-mapping, you'll use it frequently. If you have children, share the technique with them. They'll appreciate this skill when they have to write compositions for school.

Map Now, Write Later: The Joy of Mindmapping

No time to sit down and write? If you carry a notebook with you, you can always mindmap a topic for later. When my son's hamster died, I did a mindmap the same day. I tucked the mindmap in a file and forgot about it. Then I needed to show a pet page for a scrapbook magazine, so I pulled out the mind map and Ta Da! It was so easy. If you carry a notebook in your car, you could put a list of future page topics in the inside cover and mindmap inside the notebook while you wait in car pool lines at school or at the dentist. Then, rip out the mindmaps and file them by topic.

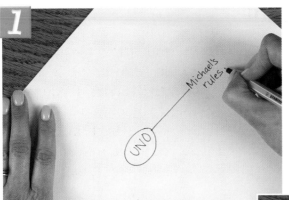

Write your topic in the center of a piece of blank paper. Draw a circle around the topic. Create spokes going out from the center circle. As quickly as possible, write thoughts that come to mind about the topic at the end of the spokes.

Circle the information at the end of the spokes. Go one by one through the circles and reconsider what you've written. Add new ideas that relate to the second set of circles.

Decide what you want to use from your mindmap and organize your thoughts. Write your material in your computer. Adjust the margins. Print out a rough draft and check it for spacing. Adjust the spacing and print out a polished copy.

Tip! Uneventful

Often scrapbookers focus on life's events: holidays, birthday parties, going special places. But you do a lot of living between special events. In fact, your daily activities are more what life is all about. Consider what uneventful happenings make up your life and resolve to scrapbook them.

Tip! Mindmap Redux

Several years ago I was in charge of a conference for our local speaker's association. I used flip chart sheets of paper to mindmap the sign-up process, the outreach plans and the various responsibilities we had to assign. Having a big sheet of paper gave me lots of room to make notes and follow tangents. Once I finished my charts, I was better prepared to streamline the information in report form. I still reach for big flip chart sheets when I have a large project to tackle.

No More Wasted Minutes—Get Journaling

Ever find yourself waiting at a restaurant for your food to arrive? Or, waiting in the pick-up line at school for your children to bounce out the door? These are prime journaling times. Grab your notebook and make a few scribbles about anything that's been on your mind. Or flip over that placemat and draw columns on the back. Fill the columns with what's been happening at your house lately. A few tips:

- Don't bother trying to write perfectly. Simply get down a few essential words or phrases.
- Don't worry about spelling, punctuation or grammar. Go fast instead. Going fast keeps the juices flowing.
- Do leave blanks for what you can't recall. A name? A date? Get someone else to help you fill in the blank later.
- Don't forget to take your notes home with you!

TOOLBOX

SUPPLIES USED

Paper:
Solid by Memories
Forever
Plaid by Provo Craft

Punch:
All Night Media

Stamp:
Clear Stamps

Ink:
ColorBox

Pen:
Milky Gel Roller by
Pentel

Template:
Journaling Genie by
Chatterbox

Other Supplies:
Photo & Document
Mending Tape by 3M

? STORY STARTERS

*What "lovies" are part
of your life? What gives
you comfort? What are
your children's prized,
never-part-with,
possessions?*

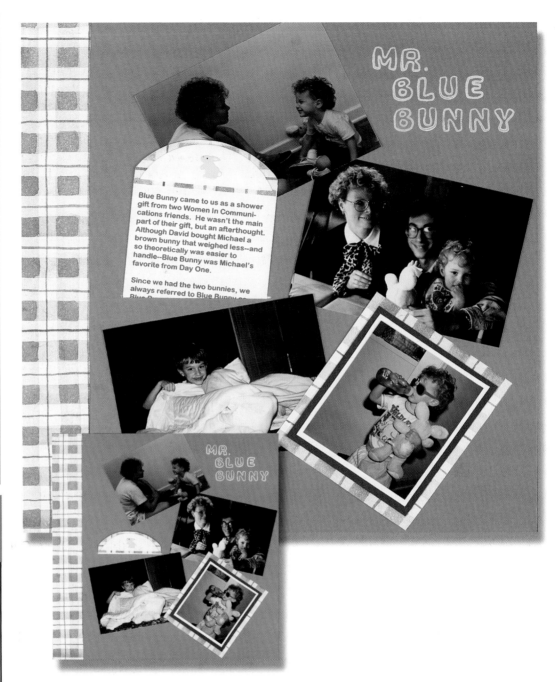

Blue Bunny came to us as a shower gift from two Women In Communications friends. He wasn't the main part of their gift, but an afterthought. Although David bought Michael a brown bunny that weighed less--and so theoretically was easier to handle--Blue Bunny was Michael's favorite from Day One.

Since we had the two bunnies, we always referred to Blue Bunny as

MR. BLUE BUNNY

Love that Lovie!

E very child needs a lovie, a blanket or creature to hold for security. Often, we forget where the lovie came from and all the adventures a lovie has.

Blue Bunny was not our choice, but he was Michael's favorite from the start. Being the first-time, know-it-all mom I was, I had planned to buy TWO of some stuffed animal so we wouldn't have to go through the agony of Lovie Loss. Are you laughing yet? As if our pre-parental plans ever happen without a hitch!

CRAFTING: *Adding a Journaling Pull Out Strip*

Cut a strip of patterned paper to run down the left side of your page. Mat your primary focus photo several times, including one mat of the patterned paper. Decide where the photos will go. Stamp on the headline in white ink. Adhere all the photos to your page.

Draw a horizontal line 3 1/4" inches long on the page. Cut it with a craft knife. Cut a rectangle of paper 4 1/2" x 6" and adhere it with archival tape to the back of the page behind the slot. This forms the pocket for your journaling strip.

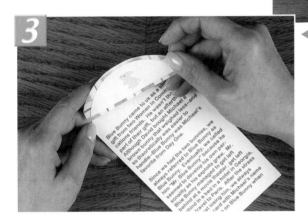

Type the journaling using 2 3/4" margins. Print it out on archival paper. Use a circular template to make a white curve. Cut it out. Use the white curve for a pattern and draw a mat on patterned paper. Cut it out. Adhere the two pieces together. Add them to top of the journaling strip. Put punch art inside the white curve. Slip it into the slot.

Where to Put Your Journaling

What do you do when you run out of room for journaling? If you leave it out, you have a photo album, not a memory book. Instead:

- **Put** journaling inside a pocket, like on this page.
- **Hinge** a photo so that it opens like a greeting card and put your journaling inside.
- **Add** a facing page and put your journaling on that page.
- **Write** around photos and add journaling directly to the page.
- **Write** inside a die cut or embellishment by cutting out the inside of the embellishment and attaching the outline to paper with your journaling written inside.

Chronological Albums

There are folks who only create albums from photos in chronological order, and there are the rest of us. I like grouping photos from different dates to show how we've changed or stayed the same as a family.

See Through Stamps

The quick headline was created on this page with Clear Stamps. Because the die (face with the image) of the stamp and the stamp handle are see-through, you can easily decide where to put your letters. In fact, you can even line up your stamp and re-stamp an image if you only get a partial print the first time. Since headlines can be time-consuming, an alphabet of Clear Stamps is a prudent investment.

WRITING: *Using the Torn Paper Technique*

How is it possible to bring order out of memory?

—Beryl Markham

Once in a while, I dump out all the contents of my purse and begin the laborious task of getting my personal baggage in order. Since a wallet is a tangible tool for storage, I can only shudder when I consider how cluttered and messy an intangible tool like my mental filing cabinet could be.

Part of what takes time when we write is conquering the clutter. Once we've spilled all the contents onto the table, how do we organize our thoughts? How do we turn random fragments into coherent stories?

Back in high school, you might have learned to copy notes for term papers onto neat index cards. The Scotswoman in me always hated the waste involved. An index card seemed too sacred to muss up, much less to throw away. When I didn't use the card for the report, I felt like a wastrel. How could I use expensive index cards to brainstorm? At least in high school, their use was teacher-mandated. But now? To scratch down ideas? That would be the ultimate in gluttony. Then, a friend taught me a cheaper and, to my mind, more practical way to snatch ideas and get them to line up in order.

First, tear a sheet of paper into little scraps about 1" x 1" in size. **Second**, brainstorm and write an idea, phrase, word or fact on each little scrap. **Third**, spread the scraps out and sort them by topic, putting them in a rough order. Add transitions where necessary. **Now** you're ready to write. The little thrifty person in you can also dance a jig!

BONUS TIP #8

I hate wasting scrapbook paper. As I work, I toss the partial sheets into a big box lid. When the lid gets full, I divide up paper into large chunks (1/4 to 1/2 of a page), strips and odd sizes. Then I cut the odd sizes into wide strips and from them I punch out tiles for tile lettering. Finally, I sort the tiles, strips and chunks of paper into gallon-size baggies by color families. It's fairly simple to do this while watching TV.

Tear paper into squares about 1" or so in size.

≈ AND ≈

Start to fill in words or phrases.

≈ AND ≈

Organize your torn pieces of paper.

Extras! Extras! Read All about Them!

What do you do if you have extra torn scraps of paper? Toss them in a ziplock bag for next time. You can write all sorts of communication with the torn paper method: letters, speeches and articles. If you have extra scraps you've written on, but that you didn't use on your page, paperclip them together and put them in an idea folder or in a page protector with photos you might want to use later. Organize your pages as you go and you're always ready to scrap. You can jot down thoughts while waiting for the buzzer on the dryer or for the timer on the microwave. One minute here, one minute there all add up. When you're ready to journal on your pages, you'll be amazed at how quickly it goes.

Fold a piece of blank paper into strips. Tear the strips. Cut the strips into small squares 1" x 1" or so. Write ideas, phrases, and or facts as quickly as possible until you don't have any more to write.

Take a Picture of Their Generosity

As your children grow and change, so will their toys. Before we take pre-loved toys to the Salvation Army, I snap a photo of Michael and his donation. The resulting picture makes him feel good immediately as well as later when he sees the page. And, I get to remember how he's grown and how his interests have changed.

Gather the pieces of paper into piles by topic. Write on additional pieces any transitions or information you may now see you are missing. Paperclip together topics if a grouping is large enough.

Type the information into your computer, going through the scraps of paper and copying them one at a time. Turn the information into sentences.

Save Memories, Clear Clutter

It's hard to say good-bye to your child's outgrown clothes, toys and hobbies. If you don't divest your home of stuff, you'll be overwhelmed by clutter. Taking photos is one painless way of moving on and clearing the decks. You could do a page of outgrown T-shirts or pajamas or board games or collector's cards or stuffed animals or school supplies. Use your scrapbook to streamline and simplify your material world.

Print out a rough draft of the journaling. Check the margins and spacing. Print out a final draft on archival paper. Trim it. Add it to the scrapbook page.

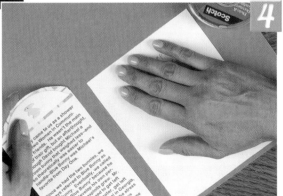

BONUS TIP #9

The easiest way to add your pocket to the back of your page is by taping it down with 3M's Photo and Document Mending Tape. I also use this tape for reinforcement, so I put it around the back side of the slot I cut just as you might reinforce a button hole when sewing.

This year I let the boys trim the Christmas tree. We bought this "pre-fit" tree from Michaels, so all the guys had to do was hang ornaments. Joon Ho was surprised by how many ornaments we had collected over the years. Kevin sat on the sofa and watched us. December, 2000

* Heart-shaped Victorian ornament trimmed in lace, made from a candy container and card.

* Hand-sewn felt mouse with thread whiskers and bead eyes and nose.

* Snowflake crocheted by Sharla Z. One of two she made for me.

* Toilet paper roll covered with felt. Meg made this Santa when she was about 10, and we were so broke! It's my absolute favorite.

? STORY STARTERS

What holiday habits have your parents passed on to you? Have you taken the time to share with your family what holiday items have special meaning for you?

TOOLBOX

SUPPLIES USED

Paper:	Solid by Memories Forever
	Winter Holidays Scrap Pads by Provo Craft
	Tree paper by Paper Adventures
Fonts:	Times Roman
Punch:	Carl
Stencil:	Alphabet Template by Frances Meyer
Other:	Oval cropper by Shaping Memories

A Time of Memories—Past and Present

Each year when I open the box of Christmas ornaments, I feel like I'm revisiting old friends. This year, I decided that I needed to document the ancestry of at least four very special trinkets that bring me joy at the holidays. As we decorated the tree, I told the boys—Michael, my son, and Joon Ho, our Korean exchange student—about my favorites. By telling the tale verbally at first, it was easier to go back and write down what I had said. Why not document your favorite possessions? It's the story behind them that makes them so special.

CRAFTING: *Making a Paper Christmas Tree*

◀ **Trace** the lettering onto the backside of the patterned paper using a lettering stencil. Cut out the letters. Affix them to solid paper and mat them with patterned paper.

Crop and **mat** the photos as desired. Silhouette crop (cut away the background) on the photos of specific items. Mat the journaling boxes. ▶

◀ **Create** the tree by cutting out a 2" x 1" trunk from brown paper. Color it with markers. Cut out two pieces of fir tree paper, shaped as much like right triangles as possible. Overlap the tree paper to make a tree. Trim out needles on the left. Mount all the elements on the page. Add ornaments. Trim any overhanging paper.

It's a Stretch

Ever run a little short of paper? I wanted to mat the journaling boxes, but the paper square was too small. So, I cut the square into strips. I mounted the strips around the journaling. Where the strips didn't meet at the corners, I added stars. You could use other embellishments—stickers, punch shapes or any design cut out of paper.

Near & Far

When you take photos, try the Near and Far approach for versatility. Here's how: Photograph your subject from far enough away to get a person and an object both in the picture. Now, photograph a close-up of the object. With these two versions of an image, you can show both scale (the object compared to the person) and detail. And, photos of people are more interesting than photos of things.

Spread the Joy Over Two Pages or More

Putting a photo in the middle of your two-page spread is just one way to visually pull two pages together. Here are a few other ideas:

- **Extend** the page title across two pages.
- **Use** the small patterned paper on both pages or use papers from the same color or pattern family.
- **Repeat** an embellishment on both pages—in this case the stars that appear in one of the papers also show up on the tree and on the corners of the journaling boxes.
- **Repeat** accent colors on both pages—especially note the strong gold that appears in the title, the stars, and the mats.

WRITING: *Warming Up with Catalog Copy*

Find a catalog with copy you'd like to emulate.

🕭 *OR* 🕭

Collect the objects you'd like to describe.

🕭 *AND* 🕭

Start to write descriptions of each object.

Frame, proportion, perspective, the values of light and shade, all are determined by the distance of the observing eye.

—Eudora Welty

The availability and relative affordability of photographs can keep us from becoming good writers. As scrapbookers, we cherish the thought that "One picture is worth a thousand words." Then we begin to lean on that thought so it becomes a crutch. Yes, a photo can say a lot. But, photos can be deceptive. Remember my Einstein page on page 46? Recently, my foreign exchange student looked at it and said, "That's Einstein—but he's DEAD."

Although Joon Ho has been learning English at a phenomenal rate, I couldn't explain what a wax figure is. We had to wait until his Korean tutor came over to get the whole situation straightened out.

The lesson? Even a clear photo can't tell the whole story. With that in mind, writing a brief but accurate description of an image is important.

And when it comes to descriptive copy, nobody does it better than the catalogs.

You see, catalog and advertising copywriters are probably the best writers out there. If their stuff isn't good, merchandise doesn't sell. If merchandise doesn't sell, they are out of a job. So when you next read a catalog or an ad, pay close attention to the style of writing. You'll see:

1) **Interesting verbs**—these convey action. For example, words like *crocheted*, *trimmed*, and *covered* are used to explain how a product is made.

2) **Concrete and specific detail**. For example, words like *felt*, *thread*, and *lace* tell you exactly what the materials are and give you a feel for their density.

Before you settle down to write, read through a few catalogs. The style will seep into your writing even without conscious effort on your part.

What Description Really Is, and What It Really Intends to Do

Aldous Huxley wrote, "The capacity for perception depends upon the amount, the kind and the availability of past experiences." For example, the more paintings I see, the more comparisons and contrasts I can draw from the differing styles and themes of each artist. When you write a descriptive passage, first compare your subject to other subjects you have encountered. Is this bigger, smaller, harder, softer, prettier, coarser, more delicate, less sturdy, and so on? Descriptions give readers the opportunity to distinguish an item or a subject from others they've known. Before you describe, think: If this item were one in a pile of similar articles, how might I pick this one out of the crowd?

◄ **Read** through catalog copy of "wish books" you admire. Leave them out as you prepare to write.

Write descriptive phrases using your actual items as inspiration. Think in terms of what an item is made of, how it is made, and where it came from. Type the information in your computer. ▶

◄ **Edit** what you write. Print it out using bullets to separate items, if desired. Compare the rough print-out to your page. Adjust the spacing, type style and ink color as necessary. Print it out on archival paper. Trim and mat it. Adhere it to the page.

Scrap Pad Glad

All these papers except the solids (dark green, white and gold) and the fir tree came from a Provo Craft Scrap Pad. And I didn't even use a quarter of the paper in the pad. Look for Scrap Pads at your scrapbook store. What a bargain! What a time-saver! What a delight!

Recycle those Baby Clothes

One Kerry from Kentucky sent this idea to my Web site: Her mother started the tradition of wrapping her Christmas ornaments in old baby clothes. Now, each year, as she unwraps the ornaments, she can reminisce about her children's younger days. Isn't that a wonderful idea?

Have a Healthy Helping of Verbs

Verbs are the vegetables of the word kingdom. By using strong, clear verbs, you eliminate the need for weak adverbs. For example:

Weak: He walked slowly across the parking lot.

Strong: He meandered across the parking lot.
He crept across the parking lot.
He moseyed across the parking lot.

Two words you rarely see in catalog copy: "It is." Beware of weak construction such as " It is," "There are," or "This is" unless you are writing Pull Out Quotes as per page 20. Of course, we all use these phrases from time to time, but usually more precise language would leave our readers with a clearer picture in their minds.

TOOLBOX

Paper:
Solid by Canson
Parchlucent by Paper Adventures

Font:
CK Leafy Capitals

Punch:
All Night Media

Pencils:
Berol

Adhesive:
Neutral pH Adhesive by Lineco Inc.

Other Supplies:
Kodak Picture Maker

? STORY STARTERS

What was your childhood like? What was your bedroom like? What have you shared with your children about your siblings?

Our Room 1963

Jane and I shared a room until our family moved to Griffith, Indiana. The wallpaper held the plaster onto the walls, and on hot summer nights we'd slide our feet along the walls because they felt cool.

At various times, this table was different colors. Mom often made paste for us out of flour and water for our craft projects. Paper dolls were my all-time favorites and I'm working on them here.

In front of our closet is a hot air register. We would linger over these registers in the winter and savor the hot air blowing up from the coal furnace in the basement.

On the back of our closet door, you can barely see the shoe bag/doll that Grandma Marge made for us.

Older Than the Hills and Younger Than Springtime

Getting older has compensations. I don't see small stuff as well as I once did, so I love getting photos enlarged. With that process comes a world as fresh and exciting as any scientist ever discovered through a microscope. Since older photos tend to be small, having them enlarged brings another world into focus. I had forgotten many of the details of our room in Vincennes until the blown-up photo on this page brought them all back to me. Growing up, I was always either reading or drawing. Seeing myself now through adult eyes, I see a child using creativity as an escape to another world.

CRAFTING: *Creating a 3-D Vellum Border*

◀ **Select** a type font and choose a light gray color. Print out the page title on white paper. Use pencils to color in the page title. Mat the title.

Print out and **trim** the journaling box. Mat the photo. ▶

Flower Arranging

Use the tip of your needle to spread apart the flowers on the thread, then tack them down with a dab of glue on a toothpick to your strip of paper. While the glue (I used Lineco's Neutral pH Adhesive) is still wet, arrange the flowers to your liking.

◀ **Cut** a strip of brown paper 1/4" x 8". Punch out the flowers from two colors of vellum. Thread a needle and run the thread through the vellum flowers, alternating the colors. Spread them on the paper. Glue the flowers down.

Kodak Picture Maker

The Kodak Picture Maker has become my new best friend. Use the "Restore " button and watch the colors in your photos look new again. The photographic paper the Picture Maker uses makes trimming and matting pictures a snap, while color photocopies are much more flimsy and easy to rip. (Shop around because Picture Maker prices vary.)

What's Your Color?—Mixing and Matching Tips

Embellishments work because they capture the colors, the shape or the feel of a page. In this case, the flowers in the wallpaper are white and tan—but the flowers on the paper strip are white and green. The flowers work for subtle reasons: Jane's blouse is ruffled like the flowers' edges, Jane is wearing white and green like the flowers, the background wallpaper is floral. As your scrapbooking progresses, you'll move away from matchy-matchy color and find new ways to amplify your pages. Not that matchy-matchy color is bad! Heck, I pour over colors of paper to find the perfect shade. But now you have other options, right?

WRITING: *Spotlight Journaling*

In the receptive mode we simply relax and allow images or impressions to come to us without choosing the details of them; we take what comes.

—Shakti Gawain

In our minds we store file after file of information that we've forgotten how to access. A forgotten smell, a taste, the brushing of a breeze across the hairs of our arms can bring a spate of memories to the conscious awareness.

When I enlarged this photo, I also made a black and white copy. Then I pretended that I had a spotlight, a circle of attention which would only illuminate a small portion of the photo at a time. As I pinpointed my focus, memories came rushing forward to take a bow. I had forgotten the wallpaper that held the crumbling plaster to the walls. I had forgotten that weird little table Mom kept painting different colors. I had forgotten the paste of flour and water that Mom made for us long before I ever knew you could buy glue at a store.

You can evoke your long-lost memories with these simple steps:

1) **Enlarge** your color photograph.

2) **Make** a black and white copy.

3) **Use** the color picture as a guide and move from place to place on the black and white copy and document what you see while adding what you recall.

4) **Save** your spotlight journaling. Use the portions you desire for journaling on your page, but hang on to what you don't use because it's bound to be the springboard for more journaling in the future.

I like writing directly on my black and white copy by drawing spokes out to the side. One scrapbooker told me—after seeing what I had done—that she was going to use her hole punch to punch a "spotlight" out of scrap paper and shift the "spotlight" over her black and white. "I think it will help me focus and concentrate," she said.

Make a black and white copy of your original photo.

ક AND ક

Start drawing lines out from the photo on which you'll write observations and memories.

ક AND ક

Write a memory or two.

My Grandmother Was Not Known for Her Patience or Her Tact

I'm amazed at what my sisters remember. Over Christmas we were talking about a time when my grandmother yelled at me in a shoe store. (My grandmother was a stinker. I loved her, but golly, she had a temper.) My sister Jane remembered the situation and her feelings of embarrassment for me in startling detail. If you get "stuck" while trying to remember, share your thinking with a sibling. What one of you doesn't recover, the other one probably will. It's funny how two or three or more people can grow up in the same house, with the same parents, and have such different experiences. Use this interfamilial diversity to your advantage.

◀ **Enlarge** your original photo as much as possible. If you can, re-store the color.

Make a black and white photocopy ▶ of the photo. "Spotlight" one small portion of the photo at a time. Draw a line coming from that portion of the photo and write down your memories. Continue around the photo. If you get stuck, move on and then go back to the place where your memories eluded you.

◀ **Input** the information you want to use for journaling into your computer. Organize the information and write your journaling copy. Print out a rough draft and check the margins. Print out a finished copy on archival paper.

Background Drama

The background in photos can be every bit as important and interesting as the subject matter. Think of all I would have lost if this photo had been cropped. That said, I love to crop photos. But then, I also take a lot more pictures than my parents ever dreamed of. The point? Think before you cut!

Daily Life is Real

Of course, you'll take photos at birthday parties, holidays and rites of passage. Do remember, however, to take a snap or two of daily life. It's the unvarnished day-to-day drum and thrum of life that shapes us. Oh, we can gussy up when we need to, but what are we like the rest of the time? When I close my eyes, I remember my loved ones in un-guarded moments. That's when we share the intimacy of our existence.

Who Are Your People?

In the South, you'll hear folks ask, "Who are your people?" Knowing *who* you came from is almost more important than knowing *where* you came from. Breeding counts, but so do the choices we make from the time we leave our family until we create a new family of our own.

Telling our children our histories helps them see us as whole beings. I'm a parent, yes, but I'm also a child, a sister, a daughter and so on. All those influences have helped to shape me. As my son sees me in all my roles and guises, he can better appreciate why I make the choices I do. And, why I encourage him and discourage him in certain behaviors. I hope he'll learn from my experiences. I think that's more likely when he knows me as a real person, who's made mistakes and tried to learn along the way, and not as an exalted icon who's never stumbled on the path.

The Shell Seeker

These are my favorite photos of Rachel. She is so unguarded that it really shows her independence and her spirit. In addition, she's a very particular person—she didn't pick up every shell, just those that appealed to her.

Rachel loves the ocean, and her favorite part is finding seashells. Florida, 1997

? STORY STARTERS

What activities totally absorb your family members. What hobbies or pastimes make them forget all sense of time and place?

TOOLBOX

SUPPLIES USED

Paint:	Delta	Pencils:	Berol
Punch:	Carl	Font:	Snell
Ink:	ColorBox	Other:	3M Packing Tape

The Story Behind the Story

The best photos, in my humble opinion, are candid shots where the subject doesn't realize she is being photographed. My niece Rachel is old enough to understand picture-taking, and often she mugs for the camera so the photos I get of her don't look natural. These pictures were unguarded. She was busy being her own unique self. Her mind was not on having her picture taken, but on finding that oh-so-elusive and perfect shell. Her concentration on her task is obvious. Of all the photos I have of her, these are my favorites.

CRAFTING: *Using a Punch Art Stencil*

Stamp sea shells in rows going from left to right on the paper. Place your stencil in the rows between the stamped shells. Dot paint onto the stencil. Repeat until the desired color and depth of color is achieved.

Straighten Up

To get straight lines going across the page:

- Use a VIP pen or a pencil to draw lines.
- Or, tape down each end of a ruler onto a grid, slide the paper underneath and use the ruler as a guide.

Print out the journaling on peach paper, including the page title. Stamp the sea shell next to the page title. Lightly shade behind and below the sea shell with gray pencil to create a shadow.

Mat the focus photo. Affix it to the left page. Trim the paper for the right hand page so it is 1/2" short on the left and right and 1" short on the top and bottom. Affix the shell pattern paper to the background paper. Affix all of the elements to the right hand page.

Paint Your Page

Delta has a line of acid-free paints perfect for use in scrapbooks. Try these with stencils and you'll be pleased with the results. You can create perfect backgrounds in the exact colors you want. The punch art stencil idea gives you yet another way to use your punches. Like you, I'm always looking for new ways to use what I've already purchased for scrapbooking.

Stenciling Fast Track How To's

To create a punch art stencil: Cut several index cards into strips 1 1/2" x 5". Tape them together to form a long strip. Flip the punch upside-down so you can see where the hole will line up. Trace the hole with a pencil. When you are happy with the position of the pencil outlines, cover the index card with packing tape. Now, punch out holes.

To stencil: Line up the stencil on the paper. Dab a small amount of paint onto a foam craft sponge or make-up sponge. Dot paint onto the stencil, making sure not to use too much paint so the paint won't run under the stencil. Repeat. When satisfied, lift the stencil straight up taking care not to smear the paint.

WRITING: *Painting a Word Portrait*

There is only one trait that marks the writer. He is always watching. It's a kind of trick of the mind and he is born with it.

—Morely Callaghan

Think about "essential nature" and come up with one word that describes your subject's essential nature.

੪ OR ੪

Looking at the photo, describe what the subject is doing.

੪ OR ੪

Consider how this person and her behavior is like or different from other people you've known.

The Saturday before Christmas I was doing a forearm stand in yoga when a fit of giggles seized me, and I came tumbling down. My mirth erupted from an upside-down glance at my T-shirt, a cat in a Santa hat with a legend reading, "Buster listened patiently to what the mice wanted for Christmas... then he ate them."

Now what the heck does this have to do with scrapbooking? The point of the t-shirt is you can't change the essential nature of a cat, can you? All of us, even those of us with two legs, have an essential nature.

When I have the chance to put together a page that portrays essential nature, I think about Buster. Looking at my niece, I pondered: "What is Rachel's essential nature and how is she expressing her nature as she picks up shells?" The answer was "Rachel likes things just so." She is a very particular child. When my nephew Josh picked up sea shells, he was into quantity, not quality. Partially smashed, chipped, broken, worm-eaten shells went into his bucket. Not so with Rachel. Each shell was carefully examined, turned over and studied. Many were discarded; few were chosen.

To create a word portrait, think "Essential nature." What one word best describes your subject?

Look at your photos with a new eye. HOW does your subject live out his or her essential nature? HOW does she perform inconsequential activities? WHAT does his manner of attention say about his essential nature?

This isn't a one-minute or a five-minute technique. Although your finished writing may take even less than 60 seconds, this is a way of looking at people—and at yourself. Instead of glancing at others quickly, passing them by, we must slow down to see, really see, who they are. And there's nothing inconsequential about that.

Life in the Time of Skepticism

Writers are cautioned, "Show, don't tell." When you tell me the party was fun, I am skeptical. When you show me by saying, "We danced all night, and no one started leaving until 2 a.m." then I understand. While you will be tempted to reduce essential nature to one word, don't stop there. Tie the activity in the photo or an activity that occurs off camera to your synopsis. WHO we are shows in a thousand little ways—WHAT we wear, HOW we hold our bodies, WHAT we eat, HOW we approach life. All this cannot be dismissed as scat. It serves to lay a trail of discovery.

Write words that describe how the subject is interacting with her environment. Now, develop words that describe the subject based on her interaction with the world around her. Concentrate on the person's essential nature.

Type your words into the computer. Explain 1) HOW these photos capture an aspect of personality; 2) WHAT those personality traits are; and 3) HOW you came to that conclusion.

Add a summary statement to fill in the WHO, WHAT, WHEN, WHERE and HOW to your page.

Wordpower

Take the time to build your vocabulary. Jot down words you don't know as you read. Or reach over and grab a dictionary when you meet a new word. *Remember:* Your children are watching. Teach them to be life-long learners.

Come from Behind

Don't be afraid to take photos from behind your subject. The most striking pictures I have do not capture a person full-face, but come at them from behind. Often, the set of the shoulders, the posture of the head, the direction of the gaze are wind-socks signaling the direction of one's thoughts.

I Finished 20 Pages at the Crop and Other Urban Myths

A woman once told me proudly, "I love to journal. I do my writing while I watch *Friends* on television." No, no, no. Once in a while we must devote attention to our lives. Finishing 20 pages at a crop is fine as long as you leave space for journaling LATER when you could think about what you really, really wanted to say. Be mindful. Take a moment to relive the moment or to simply be with your photos. Then consider: WHAT is this person doing? HOW is this important? WHAT do I want to remember about this time in our lives?

You won't always be there to narrate your scrapbook. Saving photos is only one part of the task. Your *real* job is saving the memories.

Index

Other Books for Scrapbookers and Storytellers...

ISBN: 0-9630222-8-8
128 pages (1999); $19.99

Scrapbook Storytelling
Save family stories and memories with photos, journaling and your own creativity

See how to document stories—from a quick sentence to page after scrapbook page. The book is full of ways to recover stories from the past, discover the stories in the present and create stories that light the path to the future.

With easily understood steps for documenting stories, readers can choose to combine narrative with photos, journals, memorabilia and more.

ISBN: 1-930500-01-7
80 pages (2001); $14.99

Quick & Easy Pages
Save more memories in less time

If you've ever wished you had more time to scrapbook, or didn't think you had the time to start, this is the one book you must buy. Joanna Slan shares easy ways to present photographs, pull together your pages and title any page. You'll learn over a hundred speedy scrapbooking techniques along with dozens of money-saving tips. Great how-to photos guide you through every step.

ISBN: 1-930500-01-7
80 pages (2001); $14.99

Storytelling with Rubber Stamps

Create pages that better tell your stories by using rubber stamps to make your own borders, backgrounds, embellishments, page toppers, frames and more.

You can scrapbook subjects most crafters can't because stamps give you the ability to create the supporting elements you need. You'll also learn frugal tips for affordable stamping—you'll even see how to use common household items like a pencil eraser as a stamp.

ISBN: 1-930500-04-1
208 pages (2001); $14.99

I'm Too Blessed to Be Depressed

I'm Too Blessed to be Depressed is filled with inspirational stories and journaling prompts that provide the perfect prescription for the blues.

ISBN: 0-9630222-7-X
128 pages (1998); $19.99

Creating Family Newsletters

This book contains ideas and inspiration that makes a newsletter "doable" by anyone, regardless of age or writing and design ability. Through over 123 color examples, you'll see which type of newsletter is for you—text-only, poems, photo scrapbooks, cards, letters, genealogy, e-mail or Web sites. Perfect for holidays, reunions and other family celebrations!

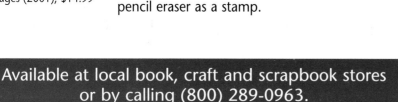

Available at local book, craft and scrapbook stores or by calling (800) 289-0963.

? STORY STARTERS

If you've enjoyed the Story Starters throughout this book, be sure to sign up at www.scrapbookstory-telling.com for my free monthly broadcast of more ideas. Click the Free Newsletter button on the home page.

This is NOT the end. It's just the beginning!

Let's keep in touch—Visit my Web site at
http://www.scrapbookstorytelling.com

There, you'll find information on the suppliers mentioned in this book, templates, new page ideas, tips and more! Plus, you'll be the first to know by e-mail about my new products, free templates, and free monthly Story Starters.

The story continues... and you can be a part of it.